# MESSAGES FROM ALLAH

## VOLUME - I

HIDAYAH PUBLISHERS

# DEAR,

_____

_____

_____

Messages From Allah – Volume I
ISBN 978-1-998843-41-1

Messages From Allah – Volume II
ISBN 978-1-998843-42-8

# List of Stories

**1** Rashid and the Tapestry of Wonders .......... 01

**2** Aleena Tames Her Anger Monster ............. 21

**3** Safiya's Big Change .......... 44

**4** Friends Fighting Shaytaan's Whispers! .63

**5** Ibrahim Learns the Power of Dua ........ 86

# RASHID
## AND THE
# TAPESTRY
## OF
# WONDERS

An Islamic Story on

Beautiful Names

of

ALLAH

# THE MYSTERIOUS TAPESTRY

Rashid was crazy about stories. He couldn't get enough of them! Every night, he'd snuggle up next to his grandma, eyes wide as saucers, as she spun tales of far-off places and super-brave heroes.

During the day, he'd curl up in his favorite squishy chair, nose buried in books about animals that could talk and magical creatures that could fly. But the best part? Rashid loved to make up his own wild stories too. He'd dream up the funniest characters and send them on the most exciting adventures. For Rashid, stories weren't just fun - they were everything!

One rainy afternoon, Rashid was feeling a bit bored. He had read all his books, and his grandmother was busy baking cookies in the kitchen. With nothing else to do, Rashid decided to explore his grandfather's attic. He had never been up there before, and he was curious about what treasures it might hold.

The attic was dusty and dim, with cobwebs hanging from the rafters. Old furniture was piled high, and boxes were stacked against the walls. Rashid carefully made his way through the clutter, his eyes searching for something interesting.

Then, in a corner, he saw it. A large tapestry, rolled up and covered in dust. Rashid's heart skipped a beat. He had never seen anything like it before. The fabric was a deep, rich blue, and it seemed to shimmer even in the dim light.

Carefully, Rashid unrolled the tapestry and spread it out on the floor. As he did, he noticed something strange. The tapestry wasn't just a picture. It was more like a window into another world. The colors were so vibrant, and the patterns so intricate, that it felt as if he could step right into the scene.

And then, something even more amazing happened. The tapestry began to shimmer and glow, and the figures within it started to move! Rashid gasped in surprise. He couldn't believe his eyes.

"Welcome, young traveler," a voice called out.

Rashid looked around, trying to find the source of the voice. Then he saw him. Woven into the fabric of the tapestry was a wise-looking old man with a long white beard and kind eyes. He wore a flowing robe and a turban on his head.

"Who are you?" Rashid asked, his voice trembling with excitement.

"I am the storyteller," the old man replied with a gentle smile. "And this," he gestured to the tapestry, "is my world. A world of stories and lessons, of wonders and wisdom."

Rashid stared at the tapestry in awe. "But how? How is this possible?"

The storyteller chuckled. "This tapestry is no ordinary cloth, young one. It is woven with threads of 'noor' and faith, and it tells the stories of Allah, the Most High."

"'Noor'?" Rashid asked, tilting his head. He had heard the name before, in the stories his grandmother told him, but he didn't quite understand.

The storyteller nodded. "Yes, Allah created 'Noor' which is like a form of light. He is the Creator of all things, the Most Merciful, the Most Compassionate. This tapestry reveals His names and attributes, teaching us about His greatness and love."

Rashid looked closer at the tapestry. He saw intricate patterns of stars and moons, mountains and rivers, flowers and trees. Each design seemed to tell a story, and he felt a deep longing to know what they meant.

"Can you tell me the stories?" Rashid asked eagerly. "Can you show me the wonders of Allah (S.W.T)?"

The storyteller smiled. "Of course, Rashid. That is why you are here. But remember," he added, his voice turning serious, "these are not just stories. They are lessons to be learned, wisdom to be gained. Each journey within this tapestry will teach you something new about yourself and about Allah (S.W.T)."

Rashid nodded, his heart filled with excitement and anticipation. He was ready for an adventure, a journey of discovery and faith.

"Where do we start?" he asked, his eyes sparkling with curiosity.

The storyteller pointed to a section of the tapestry depicting a majestic golden throne, adorned with jewels and surrounded by clouds. "Let us begin with the story of the King," he said. "The King of Kings, the Ruler of all that exists."

And with that, Rashid took a step forward and entered the world of the tapestry, ready to learn the lessons in the stories and discover the wonders that awaited him.

## MEETING THE KING

As Rashid stepped into the scene on the tapestry, he felt a rush of cool air and the faint scent of roses. He found himself standing in a magnificent courtyard, surrounded by towering marble columns and sparkling fountains. Birds chirped sweetly in the trees, and the sun shone brightly in a clear blue sky.

Before him stood a grand palace, its golden domes glinting in the sunlight. Guards in shining armor stood at attention, their faces serious and alert. Rashid felt a little nervous, but also incredibly excited. He had never seen anything so grand and beautiful.

Taking a deep breath, he walked towards the palace gates. As he approached, the guards bowed their heads respectfully.

"Welcome, young traveler," one of the guards said. "The King awaits you."

Rashid followed the guard through the palace doors and into a large hall. His eyes widened in amazement. The walls were adorned with intricate mosaics, and the floor was covered in plush carpets. Golden chandeliers hung from the ceiling, casting a warm glow over the room.

At the far end of the hall, seated upon a magnificent throne, was a wise-looking man with a beard and kind eyes. He wore a flowing robe of the finest silk and a golden crown on his head. This, Rashid knew, must be the King.

Rashid approached the throne nervously.

"Assalam-o-Alaikum, dear Rashid," the King said, his voice deep and gentle. "I have been expecting you."

"Wa Alykum Assalam, Mr. King..," Rashid stammered.

The King smiled. "Please, child, there is no need for formalities. Come, sit beside me."

Rashid climbed the steps to the throne and sat beside the King, feeling a mixture of awe and wonder.

"This is a magnificent palace," Rashid said, gazing around in amazement. "Are you the king of this land?"

The King chuckled. "This palace, with its grandeur and beauty, is meant to help you understand something far greater, Rashid. Just as you see me wearing a crown, sitting on this throne, and having servants who obey my commands, there is a King far more powerful and majestic who rules over all of creation."

Rashid's eyes widened. "You mean... there's a king even greater than you?"

The King nodded. "Yes, child. His name is Allah, and He is **Al-Malik**, the King of Kings, the Creator of the entire universe: the vast skies with countless stars, the Earth with its mountains and oceans, the sun and the moon, and even the galaxies beyond what your eyes can see. He has countless angels who fulfill His orders with perfect obedience, just as my guards obey me."

**"He is Allah—there is no god except Him: the King, the Most Holy, the All-Perfect, the Source of Serenity, the Watcher 'of all', the Almighty, the Supreme in Might, the Majestic. Glorified is Allah far above what they associate with Him 'in worship'!"**

**[Surah Al-Hashr, 59:23]**

Rashid tried to imagine the vastness of Allah's kingdom, the endless expanse of the universe, and the countless stars twinkling like tiny diamonds. It was beyond his comprehension, far grander than anything he had ever seen or imagined.

"So... everything we see around us, the trees, the animals, even us... we are all part of Allah's kingdom?" Rashid asked in awe.

"Yes, my dear," the King replied gently. "And just as you show respect to me as a king, we should all recognize Allah's authority and power by observing the wonders of His creation all around us. The rising and setting of the sun, the changing seasons, the intricate design of a tiny flower; these are all signs of His greatness and majesty."

He continued, "Think of the birds soaring in the sky, Rashid. Who taught them to build their nests and fly with such precision? Who guides the fish through the vast oceans and provides food for all living creatures? It is Allah, the Most High, who cares for His creation and ensures everything functions in perfect harmony."

Rashid looked out of the palace's gigantic window at the beautiful gardens below, the vibrant flowers swaying in the gentle breeze, and the busy bees buzzing from blossom to blossom. He thought about the squirrels he saw playing in the trees near his house and the birds singing their morning songs. He had never really thought about it before, but the King was right. Everything around him was a sign of Allah's power and wisdom.

"It's like... Allah is the biggest and best king ever!" Rashid exclaimed, his face lighting up with understanding.

The King smiled warmly. "Exactly! And as His believers, it is our duty to obey Him, to be grateful for His blessings, and to live our lives in a way that pleases Him."

# THE PURE AND THE HOLY

Whoosh! Rashid blinked and found himself in a whole new place. No more big palace or busy courtyards. Nope! Now he was standing in a quiet meadow, all sunny and peaceful. The grass was so soft under his feet, that it felt like walking on a fluffy green carpet. Pretty flowers of all colors danced in the gentle wind. The air smelled super sweet, like a big bunch of flowers, and birds were singing their happy tunes all around.

Then Rashid heard something. It sounded like water! He followed the noise and - wow! - there was a beautiful river. It looked like a long, sparkly necklace stretching across the meadow. The water was so clear, Rashid could see right through it to the little stones at the bottom.

By the riverbank, a woman sat peacefully, her eyes closed in quiet contemplation. She wore a simple white dress. Her face was kind and serene, radiating a sense of peace and tranquility that drew Rashid closer.

Hesitantly, Rashid approached the woman. "Excuse me," he said softly, not wanting to disturb her peaceful meditation.

The woman opened her eyes and smiled warmly at Rashid.

"Welcome, kid," she said, her voice as gentle as the flowing water. "What brings you to this peaceful place?"

"I'm Rashid," he replied, feeling instantly at ease in her presence. "I'm on a journey through the Storyteller's tapestry, learning about the names of Allah (S.W.T)."

"Ah, a noble pursuit," the woman said. "And what have you learned so far?"

"I met the King," Rashid said excitedly, "and he taught me about Allah's power and authority over all creation. He is Al-Malik, the King of Kings!"

The woman nodded. "Yes, Allah is indeed the Ruler of all that exists. But He is also **Al-Quddus**, the Pure, the Holy." She gestured towards the river. "Just as this river flows with pure and clear water, so too does Allah's essence radiate with perfect purity and holiness."

"Whatever is in the heavens and whatever is on the earth 'constantly' glorifies Allah—the King, the Most Holy, the Almighty, the All-Wise." [Surah Al-Jumu'ah, 62:1]

The Messenger of Allah (P.B.U.H) said, "O people! Allah is Pure and, therefore, accepts only that which is pure. ..." (Reported by Muslim)

Rashid looked at the river, observing how the water cleansed everything it touched. Leaves that fell into the stream were carried away, and even the rocks seemed to gleam brighter after being washed by the flowing water.

"The river is like... a symbol of cleanliness," Rashid observed thoughtfully.

The woman smiled. "Exactly! And just as the river cleanses the earth, so too does striving for purity cleanse our hearts and souls, bringing us closer to Allah."

She explained to Rashid that purity was not just about physical cleanliness, like washing our hands and bodies. It was also about having a pure heart, free from bad thoughts and intentions. It meant speaking kind words, doing good deeds, and always striving to be the best version of ourselves.

"But how can we keep our hearts pure?" Rashid asked, furrowing his brow. "Sometimes I get angry or say things I shouldn't."

The woman placed a gentle hand on his shoulder. "We all make mistakes, Rashid. That is part of being human. But Allah is Most Forgiving and Merciful. He knows our struggles, and He wants us to turn to Him for guidance and forgiveness."

She explained that through sincere repentance and striving to do good deeds, we can cleanse our hearts and draw closer to Allah. Just like the river washes away dirt and debris, Allah's forgiveness washes away our sins and allows us to start anew.

"Remember," the woman said, "Allah loves those who purify themselves. He says in the Quran,

"Surely Allah loves those who always turn to Him in repentance and those who purify themselves."

[Al-Baqarah, 2:222]

Rashid felt a warmth spread through his heart as he listened to the woman's words. He realized that striving for purity was not just a duty, but a way to express his love for Allah and earn His pleasure.

"But what kind of deeds can I do to be pure?" Rashid asked eagerly.

The woman's smile widened. "Oh, there are countless ways, dear child! You can help your parents with chores, share your toys with your friends, speak kindly to others, and always try your best to be honest and truthful. Even small acts of kindness can make a big difference."

## THE CROSSROADS OF CHOICE

Rashid took in the wise words from the woman and thanked her before stepping into the next scene on the tapestry. The peaceful meadow and the gentle river were gone. Instead, he found himself standing at a crossroads, with two distinct paths stretching out before him.

One path was wide and smooth, paved with glittering gold and lined with fragrant flowers. People strolled along this path with carefree smiles, indulging in delicious food, playing games, and laughing merrily. The air buzzed with music and the sounds of celebration.

The other path was narrow and rocky, winding its way up a steep hill. It was a difficult path, with thorny bushes and sharp stones, and the people walking on it seemed tired and burdened. Some carried heavy loads on their backs, while others limped with injuries. Yet, despite their hardships, there was a look of determination in their eyes, and many whispered prayers as they journeyed onward.

Rashid felt confused. He didn't know which path to choose. The first path seemed so inviting and easy, full of fun and enjoyment. But the second path, though difficult, seemed to lead somewhere important, somewhere meaningful.

"Which path should I take?" Rashid asked the storyteller, who had appeared beside him once again.

The storyteller pointed towards the two paths. "These paths represent the choices we make in life, young Rashid. One path is the path of ease and self-indulgence, where people follow their desires and forget about their obligations to Allah. The other is the path of righteousness and struggle, where people strive to obey Allah and live according to His guidance, even when it's difficult."

Rashid looked at the people on the first path. They seemed happy and carefree, but there was also a sense of emptiness in their eyes. He noticed that they ignored the needs of others, focused only on their own pleasure and enjoyment.

He then looked at the people on the second path. They faced many challenges, but there was a sense of peace and purpose in their faces. They helped each other along the way, sharing their burdens and offering words of encouragement.

"Why would anyone choose the difficult path?" Rashid asked, still feeling unsure.

The storyteller sighed. "Many people are deceived by the allure of worldly pleasures, young Rashid. They forget about the Hereafter and the consequences of their actions. They think that happiness can be found in material possessions and self-gratification, but true happiness comes from pleasing Allah and living a life of purpose."

He explained that Allah has given us free will, the ability to choose between right and wrong. We can choose to follow our desires and ignore Allah's guidance, but this ultimately leads to loss and regret in the Hereafter. Or we can choose to obey Allah, even when it's difficult, and earn His pleasure and eternal rewards in Paradise.

"Allah says in the Quran,

"**Whoever does good, whether male or female, and is a believer, We will surely bless them with a good life, and We will certainly reward them according to the best of their deeds.**"

[Surah An-Nahl, 16:97]

Rashid watched as some people on the first path stumbled and fell, their laughter turning into cries of despair. They had reached a dead end, a place of darkness and hopelessness.

He then saw others who started on the first path but eventually realized their mistake. With regret in their hearts, they turned back and joined those on the difficult path, seeking forgiveness and a chance to start anew.

"What happens to those who choose the wrong path?" Rashid asked, his voice filled with concern.

The storyteller's expression turned serious. "Those who reject Allah's guidance and persist in disobedience will face the consequences of their actions on the Day of Judgement. They will be held accountable for every deed, every word, and even every thought."

He explained that Allah, in His infinite justice and mercy, has prepared a place called Hell for those who continue to disobey Him and cause harm to others. It is a place of fire and torment, a consequence of their own choices.

"But Allah is also Most Merciful," the storyteller added. "He always gives people a chance to repent and return to the right path. Even those who have made many mistakes can earn His forgiveness through sincere repentance and good deeds."

> "Say, 'O Prophet, that Allah says,' O My servants who have exceeded the limits against their souls! Do not lose hope in Allah's mercy, for Allah certainly forgives all sins. He is indeed the All-Forgiving, Most Merciful."
>
> [Surah Az-Zumar, 39:53]

Rashid felt a mix of emotions as he observed the choices people made and the consequences they faced. He felt empathy for those who struggled and made mistakes, but he also felt a sense of responsibility to make the right choices in his own life.

# THE BALANCE OF AWE AND LOVE

Filled with a new determination to do the right thing, Rashid continued his journey through the Storyteller's tapestry. With each step, he entered a new scene, discovered a new story, and learned a new lesson about Allah's names and qualities.

He met a wise old farmer who taught him about **Ar-Razzaq** (The Provider), the One who sustains all living beings with food and nourishment. He learned about the importance of hard work, patience, and gratitude for the blessings of the earth.

Then he encountered a skilled craftsman who taught him about **Al-Musawwir** (The Shaper), the One who creates with perfect artistry and design. Rashid marveled at the intricate details of the craftsman's work, understanding that everything in creation, from the smallest insect to the vast galaxies, is a testament to Allah's artistry and wisdom.

He listened to a scholar who spoke of **Al-Alim** (The All-Knowing), the One who possesses infinite knowledge and understanding. He learned about the importance of seeking knowledge, reflecting on the wonders of creation, and striving to understand Allah's wisdom.

With each story, Rashid's understanding of Allah deepened. He realized that Allah is not just a King or a powerful Creator, but also a close and loving companion, always present and aware of his every thought and action.

One day, as Rashid stood before a scene depicting a vast starry sky, he turned to the storyteller with a question that had been lingering in his mind.

"Storyteller," he asked, "I understand that Allah is all-powerful and majestic, but I also feel a sense of closeness to Him, a feeling of love and comfort. How can both be true?"

The storyteller smiled knowingly. "Ah, young Rashid, you have come to understand one of the most beautiful aspects of our relationship with Allah; the balance between His authority and His closeness."

He explained that Allah's names and attributes encompass both His grandeur and His intimacy. Names like **Al-Malik** (The King) and **Al-Jabbar** (The Compeller) remind us of His absolute power and authority, inspiring awe and reverence. But names like **Ar-Rahman** (The Most Compassionate) and **Al-Wadud** (The Loving) reveal His immense love and mercy, drawing us closer to Him with feelings of love and trust.

"This balance is essential," the storyteller continued. "If we only focused on Allah's power and authority, we might become overwhelmed with fear and lose hope. But if we only focused on His closeness and love, we might become too casual and forget the respect and obedience He deserves."

Rashid thought about the King he had met in the palace, and how he embodied both authority and compassion. He realized that true leadership, whether among humans or in the divine realm, involved a delicate balance between power and love, justice and mercy.

"So, we should both fear and love Allah (S.W.T)?" Rashid asked, trying to grasp this complex concept.

The storyteller nodded. "Yes, Rashid. We should fear His punishment and strive to avoid His displeasure, but we should also love Him for His infinite mercy and the countless blessings He bestows upon us. This balance will guide us towards a healthy and meaningful relationship with our Creator."

**"And call upon Him with hope and fear. Indeed, Allah's mercy is always close to the good-doers."**

**[Surah Al-A'raf, 7:56]**

As Rashid continued his journey, he began to see the tapestry not just as a collection of stories, but as a reflection of life itself. The intricate patterns and interconnected threads represented the complexity and interconnectedness of all creation, each element playing a vital role in Allah's grand design.

He realized that the lessons he was learning were not just about Allah (S.W.T), but also about himself and his place in the world. He understood the importance of making responsible choices, striving for purity, and living a life of purpose and meaning.

Finally, the time came for Rashid to leave the Storyteller's tapestry. He emerged from the attic, feeling transformed by his experiences. The world around him seemed brighter, more vibrant, and filled with hidden wonders. He saw the signs of Allah's presence everywhere; in the gentle breeze rustling the leaves, in the intricate patterns of a spider's web, in the smiling faces of people around him.

Rashid knew that his journey of learning and discovery was just beginning. He carried the stories and lessons of the tapestry in his heart, and he was eager to share them with others. He wanted to inspire his friends, his family, and everyone he met to explore the beauty of Allah's names and attributes, and to experience the joy of a life connected to the Divine.

# ALEENA
## TAMES HER
# ANGER
# MONSTER

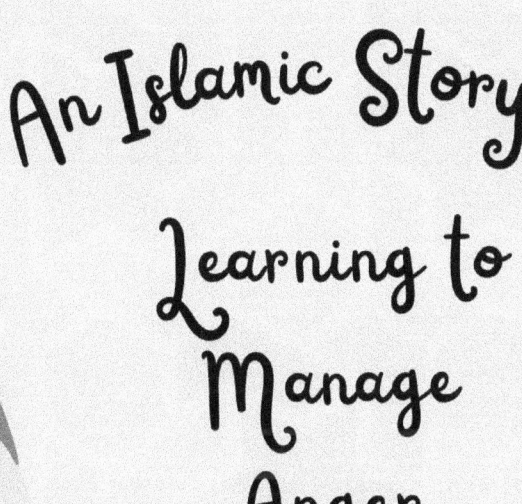

An Islamic Story on

Learning to

Manage

Anger

# THE SPARK

Aleena was a ray of sunshine. With her bright eyes and a smile that could light up a room, she brought joy wherever she went. Everyone loved Aleena; her parents, her friends, even the grumpy old cat who lived next door. She was always ready to jump in and help out. She'd say nice things to make people feel better and lend a hand faster than you could say "Let me help!" Yep, Aleena was pretty special!

One sunny afternoon, Aleena was playing with her little brother, Amir. Amir was building a tall tower with his colorful blocks, his tongue sticking out in concentration. Aleena carefully handed him each block, making sure the tower stood strong and steady.

"Look, Aleena! It's a castle!" Amir exclaimed, his eyes sparkling with excitement.

Aleena grinned. "It's a magnificent castle, Amir! Fit for a prince like you."

Suddenly, the tower wobbled and crashed to the ground, scattering blocks everywhere. Amir's face crumpled, and he started to cry.

"Don't worry, Amir," Aleena said gently, gathering the blocks. "We can build it again, even taller this time!"

But Amir was too upset. He stomped his feet and shouted, "No! I don't want to play anymore!"

He ran away, leaving Aleena feeling a strange pang in her chest. It wasn't sadness; it was something hotter, something sharper. It felt like a small spark had ignited inside her.

Later that day, Aleena was playing hopscotch with her friends, Layla and Khadijah. The girls were taking turns, hopping and jumping from square to square. Their giggles filled the air as they wobbled and tried not to step on the lines. Aleena almost fell over when she had to stand on one foot, making everyone laugh even harder.

"It's my turn!" Aleena exclaimed, ready to jump.

But Layla accidentally stepped on the line just as Aleena was about to hop.

"You cheated!" Aleena shouted, her voice louder than she intended. The spark inside her flared, growing into a small flame.

Layla's eyes widened in surprise. "I didn't mean to," she mumbled, looking down at her feet.

"You always mess things up!" Aleena's voice trembled with anger. The flame inside her grew hotter, making her face feel flushed.

Khadijah stepped between them, her voice calm. "It's just a game, Aleena. Let's start again."

But Aleena couldn't let it go. She felt angry at Layla, at the game, at everything. The flame inside her roared, turning into a raging fire. She stormed off, leaving her friends staring after her in confusion.

The next day, Aleena's anger followed her like a shadow. When her mother asked her to clean her room, Aleena snapped, "Why do I always have to do everything?"

The fire inside her burned, making her feel restless and irritable. Everything seemed to annoy her; the sound of the television, the chirping of birds outside her window, even the way her brother chewed his food.

That night, tucked in bed, Aleena stared at the ceiling. Tears rolled down her cheeks, but not because she was sad. She felt all mixed up inside, a jumble of shame and confusion.

"Why am I so angry?" she whispered to herself. "This isn't who I am."

She remembered the joy of building castles with Amir, the laughter she shared with Layla and Khadijah. Now, a dark cloud seemed to hang over her, making it hard to see the sunshine.

Just then, her mother entered the room and sat beside her on the bed. She gently brushed away Aleena's tears and held her close.

"What's wrong, my dear Aleena?" she asked softly.

Aleena hesitated, then poured out her heart. She spoke of her anger, her confusion, and the fear that she was turning into someone she didn't recognize.

Her mother listened patiently, with understanding in her eyes. "Everyone feels angry sometimes," she said. "It's a normal emotion, like happiness or sadness."

Aleena looked up at her mother. "But why am I so angry all the time? I don't want to be like this anymore."

"There might be something more to it," her mother said thoughtfully. "Perhaps we should seek guidance from Sheikh Ali. He's very wise and has helped many people with their problems."

The idea of talking to Sheikh Ali, the respected elder in their community, filled Aleena with a mixture of apprehension and hope. She wasn't sure if he could help, but she was willing to try anything to extinguish the fire that raged within her.

"Will you come with me, Mama?" Aleena asked, her voice small.

Her mother smiled warmly and squeezed her hand. "Of course, my dear. We'll find answers together."

As they drifted off to sleep, Aleena felt a sense of relief. The storm within her hadn't calmed completely, but for the first time in days, she saw a sliver of light peeking through the dark clouds. She knew the journey to understanding her anger wouldn't be easy, but with her mother by her side and the hope of Sheikh Ali's guidance, she was ready to face the challenge.

# SEEKING SHEIKH ALI's WISDOM

The next morning, Aleena and her mother walked hand-in-hand to Sheikh Ali's house. Aleena's heart thumped in her chest like a little drum. She wasn't sure what to expect, but the warm sun and the gentle breeze calmed her nerves a little.

Sheikh Ali lived in a small, cozy house with a beautiful small garden filled with colorful flowers and buzzing bees. He greeted them with a kind smile and twinkling eyes that seemed to hold ancient wisdom.

"Welcome, Aleena and dear sister," he said in a gentle voice. "Please, come in and make yourselves comfortable."

Aleena and her mother sat on soft cushions in a room filled with books. Aleena felt a sense of peace, like the calm after a storm.

"So, Aleena," Sheikh Ali began, "tell me, what troubles your heart?"

Aleena took a deep breath and told him everything. She spoke about the anger that had taken hold of her, the way it made her lash out at her family and friends, and the confusion and shame she felt.

Sheikh Ali listened patiently, nodding his head in understanding. When she finished, he said, "Aleena, you are not alone in this struggle. We all face challenges and difficult emotions in life."

He paused for a moment, then continued, "Have you ever heard of Shaytaan or Satan?"

Aleena shook her head. "Yes, Sheikh. But I don't know much."

"Shaytaan is a creature who whispers negative thoughts into our hearts," Sheikh Ali explained. "He tries to lead us astray and make us do bad things. He especially likes to provoke anger within us, making us say and do things we later regret."

Aleena's eyes widened in surprise. "So, it's not just me? There's someone... or something... making me angry?"

Sheikh Ali smiled gently. "In a way, yes. But remember, Aleena, Shaytaan can only whisper. He cannot force us to do anything. We have the power to choose how we react to his whispers."

He reached for a book on a nearby shelf. "The Quran, our holy book, tells us many stories about Shaytaan and how he tries to tempt people. Allah (S.W.T) warned believers about this numerous times in the Quran. Listen to these Ayaat:

"Surely Satan is an enemy to you, so take him as an enemy. He only invites his followers to become inmates of the Blaze."

[Surah Fatir, 35:6]

"O believers! Enter into Islam wholeheartedly and do not follow Satan's footsteps. Surely he is your sworn enemy."

[Surah Al-Baqarah, 2:208]

Aleena listened carefully.

Sheikh Ali told her the story of Prophet Adam (A.S) and his wife, Hawa, and how Shaytaan tricked them into disobeying Allah.

As she listened to the story, Aleena began to understand that even the best of people could be tempted by Shaytaan's whispers. It wasn't a sign of weakness, but rather a test of faith and strength.

"So, what can I do to stop Shaytaan from making me angry?" Aleena asked, feeling a flicker of hope.

Sheikh Ali explained, "The first step is to recognize his whispers. When you feel anger rising, ask yourself, 'Is this thought coming from Allah, or is it Shaytaan trying to trick me?'"

He explained that negative thoughts like "It's not fair!" or "They always do this to me!" were often whispers from Shaytaan. He encouraged Aleena to replace these thoughts with positive ones, like "I can handle this calmly" or "Allah is with me, and He will help me through this."

"It's like having two little birds on your shoulders," Sheikh Ali said, smiling. "One whispers negative thoughts, and the other whispers positive ones. You get to choose which bird you listen to."

Aleena closed her eyes and imagined two tiny birds perched on her shoulders. One was dark and scruffy, whispering angry words, while the other was bright and cheerful, singing songs of hope and peace.

"I want to listen to the good bird," Aleena said with determination.

Sheikh Ali nodded with a smile. "That's the spirit, Aleena. Remember, you have the power to control your thoughts and emotions. With Allah's help, you can overcome Shaytaan's whispers and find peace within yourself."

"Jazak Allah, Sheikh!" Yasmeen thanked him with a smile.

"Tomorrow, I'll teach you some duas to recite when you feel angry," Sheikh Ali said as he bid them farewell.

Walking away from Sheikh Ali's house, Aleena felt like even the sun was smiling! A little breeze tickled the leaves, and she imagined it blowing away all the grumpy whispers. She felt brave, ready to tackle her anger, even though she knew it wouldn't be easy peasy. With her family and Sheikh Ali beside her, Aleena was ready to let her own inner sunshine blaze!

# THE POWER OF DUA

The days that followed were filled with learning and practice for Aleena. Sheikh Ali taught her about the power of seeking refuge in Allah, the One who protects and guides us. He explained that when Shaytaan whispers negative thoughts, we can turn to Allah for help and strength.

"Allah is always with us, Aleena," Sheikh Ali said. "He hears our prayers and knows what's in our hearts. When we seek refuge in Him, He gives us the strength to overcome our challenges."

"If you are tempted by Satan, then seek refuge with Allah. Surely He is All-Hearing, All-Knowing. Indeed, when Satan whispers to those mindful 'of Allah', they remember 'their Lord' then they start to see 'things' clearly."

[Surah Al-A'raf, 7:200-201]

Sheikh Ali taught Aleena some special duas, or supplications, that she could recite whenever she felt anger bubbling up inside her. One of the duas was:

"A'udhu billahi minash-Shaytaanir rajeem."

This means: "I seek refuge in Allah from Shaytaan, the rejected one."

Aleena practiced saying the dua over and over again until the words rolled off her tongue instantly in difficult situations.

Another dua Sheikh Ali taught her was:

"My Lord, I seek refuge in You from the incitements of the devils, and I seek refuge in You, my Lord, lest they come near me."

Aleena loved how these duas made her feel. When she recited them, it was as if a shield of protection formed around her, keeping Shaytaan's whispers at bay. She started incorporating them into her daily routine, saying them before she went to school, before she played with her friends, and especially when she felt the first sparks of anger ignite within her.

One afternoon, Aleena was playing a board game with Amir. They were having fun at first, but then Amir started getting frustrated because he wasn't winning. He began to pout and kick his feet against the table, making the game pieces wobble.

Aleena felt that familiar spark of anger ignite within her. *"Amir, stop it!" she wanted to shout. "You're being a sore loser!"*

But then she remembered Sheikh Ali's words and the duas she had learned. She closed her eyes for a moment and whispered, "A'udhu billahi minash-Shaytaanir rajeem."

The anger subsided a little, replaced by a sense of calm. Aleena took a deep breath and said to Amir in a gentle voice, "It's okay if you don't win, Amir. We're just playing for fun, remember?"

Amir looked up at his sister, surprised by her calm response. He stopped kicking his feet and mumbled an apology. Aleena smiled and ruffled his hair.

"Let's keep playing," she said. "And remember, it's not about winning or losing, it's about having fun together."

As they continued playing, Aleena noticed a gradual change within herself. The bursts of anger that used to erupt like volcanoes were becoming less frequent and less intense. She was learning to control her emotions and respond to situations with patience and understanding.

There were still moments when frustration crept in, like when she spilled her milk at breakfast or couldn't find her favorite book. But now, instead of letting the anger take over, she would take a deep breath, recite her duas, and remind herself that Allah is with her, guiding her every step of the way.

Aleena felt a deep sense of gratitude for Sheikh Ali's guidance and the power of faith. She realized that her anger wasn't something to be ashamed of, but rather an opportunity to grow stronger and closer to Allah. With each passing day, she felt the storm within her calming, replaced by a sense of peace and serenity.

She knew that managing her anger was an ongoing journey, but she was determined to continue practicing the lessons she had learned. And with Allah's help, she was confident that she could overcome any challenge and let her true, kind spirit shine through.

# LEARNING FROM THE BEST

Aleena continued her visits to Sheikh Ali, eager to learn more about managing her anger and strengthening her faith. One sunny afternoon, as they sat in his peaceful garden, Sheikh Ali said, "Aleena, today I want to tell you stories about some of the best people who ever lived."

Aleena's eyes sparkled with curiosity. "Who are they, Sheikh Ali?"

"They are the companions of Prophet Muhammad (peace be upon him)," Sheikh Ali replied. "They were his closest friends and followers, and they faced many challenges and hardships with incredible patience and wisdom."

He began by telling Aleena about Abu Bakr, a kind and gentle man who was always the first to believe in the Prophet (P.B.U.H) and support him. He faced ridicule and opposition from others, but remained steadfast in his faith, always responding with calmness and reason.

Next, Sheikh Ali spoke of Umar, a strong and courageous man who was known for his justice and fairness. He was once a fierce opponent of Islam, but after hearing the Quran, he embraced the faith and became one of its strongest defenders.

Aleena listened intently, her heart filled with admiration for these remarkable individuals. She learned how they faced moments of anger and frustration, but always chose to respond with patience, kindness, and forgiveness.

One story that particularly touched Aleena was the story of the Treaty of Hudaibiya. The Prophet Muhammad (P.B.U.H) and his companions had set out on a peaceful journey to perform Hajj, the pilgrimage to Mecca. However, they were stopped by their enemies and prevented from entering the city.

The companions were understandably upset. They had traveled a long way and were eager to fulfill their religious duty. Some of them felt angry and wanted to fight, but the Prophet (P.B.U.H) chose a different path. He negotiated a treaty with their enemies, even though it contained some terms that seemed unfair to the Muslims.

Aleena couldn't imagine how difficult it must have been for the companions to accept this treaty, but they followed the Prophet's example and chose peace over conflict.

"Why did the Prophet Muhammad (P.B.U.H) agree to the treaty if it wasn't fair?" Aleena asked, her brow furrowed in confusion.

"The Prophet (P.B.U.H) knew that sometimes, patience and compromise are more important than immediate victory," Sheikh Ali explained. "He had faith that Allah had a plan, and that even though things seemed difficult at the time, good would come out of it in the end."

And indeed, the Treaty of Hudaibiya turned out to be a turning point for the Muslims. It led to a period of peace and allowed Islam to spread more rapidly than ever before.

Aleena realized that even the best of people, like the Prophets of Allah and his companions, experienced anger. But what set them apart was their ability to control their emotions and respond in a way that was pleasing to Allah.

"I want to be like them," Aleena said with determination. "I want to be patient and kind, even when I feel angry."

Sheikh Ali smiled warmly. "You can be, Aleena. Remember, we all have the potential for greatness within us. By following the example of the Prophet Muhammad (P.B.U.H) and his companions, and by seeking refuge in Allah, we can overcome our challenges and become the best versions of ourselves."

Aleena left Sheikh Ali's house feeling inspired and connected. She realized that she was part of a larger community, a community of believers who had faced similar struggles throughout history. She felt a sense of belonging and a renewed determination to follow in the footsteps of those who had come before her.

As she walked home, she imagined herself as one of the Prophet's companions, facing challenges with courage and grace. She knew that there would still be times when she felt angry, but now she had the tools and the inspiration to choose a better path. And with each step she took, she felt herself growing closer to Allah and becoming the kind, compassionate person she always wanted to be.

# NURTURING THE GARDEN OF PATIENCE

One day, Aleena was visiting Sheikh Ali. She sat in his backyard, which was bursting with colorful flowers! Bees buzzed around, butterflies flitted from petal to petal, and the sun beamed down on it all.

"Your garden is so beautiful, Sheikh!" Aleena exclaimed, her eyes wide with wonder. "How do you keep it looking so lovely?"

Sheikh Ali smiled. "It takes patience, Aleena, just like controlling your anger. A garden doesn't grow overnight. It requires constant care, nurturing, and attention."

"And hasten towards forgiveness from your Lord and a Paradise as vast as the heavens and the earth, prepared for those mindful 'of Allah'. 'They are' those who donate in prosperity and adversity, control their anger, and pardon others. And Allah loves the good-doers."

[Surah Ali 'Imran, 3:133-134]

He explained that just as a gardener pulls out weeds and waters the plants, we need to remove negative thoughts and cultivate positive ones in our minds.

"Think of your heart like a garden, Aleena," Sheikh Ali said. "When you feel angry, it's like a weed sprouting up. If you let it grow, it will take over and choke the beautiful flowers of kindness, patience, and love. Remember these sayings of our Beloved Prophet (P.B.U.H):

The Messenger of Allah (P.B.U.H) said, "The person who is strong is not strong because he can knock people down. The person who is strong is the one who controls himself when he is angry." [Reference: Al-Adab Al-Mufrad 1317]

"Whoever controls his anger at the time when he has the means to act upon it, Allah will fill his heart with contentment on the Day of Resurrection." [Al-Tabarani, 12/453]

Aleena pondered his words, imagining her heart as a garden. She envisioned pulling out the prickly weeds of anger and replacing them with vibrant flowers of understanding and compassion.

Sheikh Ali taught her some simple techniques to help her nurture her "garden of patience." One of them was deep breathing.

"When you feel angry," he explained, "take a slow, deep breath in through your nose, filling your belly with air like a balloon. Then, slowly breathe out through your mouth, like you're blowing out a candle."

Aleena practiced the deep breathing exercise with Sheikh Ali, feeling her body relax with each exhale. It was like letting go of the tension and frustration that had been building up inside her.

He also told her this hadith of the Prophet Muhammad (P.B.U.H):

"If any of you becomes angry and he is standing, let him sit down, so his anger will go away; if it does not go away, let him lie down."

Another method Sheikh Ali taught her was counting to ten.

"Sometimes," he said, "we need to give ourselves a moment to calm down before we react to a situation. Counting to ten gives you time to think clearly and choose a better response."

Aleena found this technique especially helpful when dealing with her brother, Amir. He could be quite a handful sometimes, but instead of yelling at him, she would take a deep breath and count to ten. By the time she reached ten, her anger had usually subsided, and she could respond to Amir with patience and understanding.

One day, Aleena and her friends were playing hide-and-seek in the park. Aleena was counting, covering her eyes with her hands and reciting the numbers slowly. Suddenly, she heard Layla giggling nearby.

Aleena felt a surge of frustration. *"Layla, you're not hiding properly!" she wanted to shout. "You're supposed to be quiet!"*

But then she remembered her "garden of patience." She took a deep breath, counted to ten, and then said calmly, "Layla, please try to be quieter. It's not fun if I can hear you."

Layla immediately stopped giggling and found a better hiding spot. Aleena continued counting, feeling proud of herself for controlling her anger.

As Aleena practiced these techniques, she noticed a remarkable change in her relationships. Her friends enjoyed playing with her more because she wasn't so quick to anger. Her parents were happy to see her calmer and more patient. Even Amir seemed to be less mischievous, perhaps sensing his sister's newfound peace.

Aleena felt a sense of accomplishment and pride as she nurtured her "garden of patience." She realized that controlling her anger wasn't about suppressing her emotions, but rather about choosing how to respond to them. And by choosing patience, understanding, and forgiveness, she was creating a beautiful garden within herself and spreading its fragrance to those around her.

She knew that there would always be challenges, and moments when weeds of anger might try to sprout up again. But now, she had the tools and the determination to keep her garden blooming, creating a life filled with peace, happiness, and love.

# SHARING THE GIFT OF PEACE

One afternoon, as the golden rays of the setting sun painted the sky with vibrant hues of orange and pink, Aleena turned to Sheikh Ali and said with gratitude, "Thank you for everything you've taught me, Sheikh. You've helped me understand my anger and shown me how to find peace within myself."

Sheikh Ali smiled warmly. "It is Allah who guides us, Aleena. I am merely a vessel through which His wisdom flows. He says in the Quran:

'If it were not for God's bounty and mercy towards you, not one of you would ever have attained purity. God purifies whoever He will: God is all-hearing, all-seeing.' [Surah An-Nur, 24:21]."

Aleena reflected on her journey. She remembered the days when anger consumed her, turning her into someone she didn't recognize. But with Sheikh Ali's guidance and the power of faith, she had learned to tame the storm within and cultivate a garden of patience in her heart.

"I want to share what I've learned," Aleena said. "Maybe I can help other kids understand their anger and find peace, too!"

Sheikh Ali nodded encouragingly. "That is a noble goal, Aleena. Sharing your story can inspire others and give them hope."

Aleena began by sharing her experiences with her family. She sat down with her parents and Amir, explaining how Shaytaan's whispers had fueled her anger and how she had learned to overcome them with the help of Sheikh Ali's teachings.

Her parents listened attentively, their faces beaming with pride. Amir, who had witnessed his sister's transformation firsthand, promised to try his best to control his temper tantrums.

Next, Aleena shared her story with her friends at school. During recess, she gathered Layla, Khadijah, and a few other classmates under the shade of a large oak tree.

She spoke openly about her struggles with anger and the techniques she had learned to manage it. She explained the concept of Shaytaan's whispers and the importance of seeking refuge in Allah.

Her friends listened with rapt attention, some nodding in understanding, others surprised by her honesty and courage.

"I used to get angry a lot, too," Layla confessed. "But I never knew why, or what to do about it."

"Me too," Khadijah added. "I thought it was just something I had to live with."

Aleena smiled. "We don't have to live with anger controlling us. We can choose to be kind, patient, and understanding. And if we struggle, we can always seek help from Allah and those who care about us."

Her words resonated with her friends, planting seeds of hope and inspiration in their hearts. They promised to try the techniques

Aleena had shared and to support each other on their journeys towards inner peace.

As the days turned into weeks and weeks into months, Aleena continued to practice the lessons she had learned. She knew that managing anger was an ongoing effort, like tending a garden, but she was committed to nurturing her "garden of patience" and keeping it free from the weeds of negativity.

Her life transformed in beautiful ways. She experienced a deep sense of inner peace and joy that radiated outwards, touching the lives of everyone around her. Her relationships with her family and friends grew stronger, built on a foundation of love, understanding, and mutual respect.

Her heart, once a battleground of emotions, had become a garden of peace, blooming with kindness, compassion, and love. As she continued her journey, she knew that the seeds of peace she had planted would continue to blossom, creating a more beautiful and harmonious world for all.

# SAFIYA'S BIG CHANGE

An Islamic Story on

Preparing Ourselves

for

Jannah

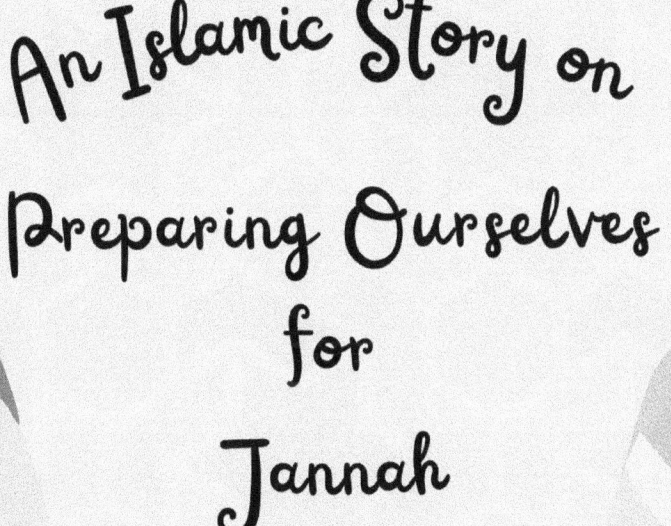

# MEETING THE BUTTERFLY

Rise and shine! It's a brand new day in the most amazing garden ever. This place is bursting with flowers of every color you can imagine, and the leaves are so green they make broccoli jealous. Right in the middle of all this awesomeness is Safiya, a tiny caterpillar who's just waking up. She gives a big stretch (well, big for a caterpillar) and lets out a teeny-tiny yawn.

Safiya thinks this garden is the best thing ever. Every day is like a new adventure for her. She munches on yummy leaves and slurps up flower juice like it's the world's tastiest smoothie. There's always something cool to check out, and Safiya never gets bored.

Today, Safiya decides to go exploring. She inches along the branches, checking out all the cool colors and crazy patterns on the leaves. But when she gets to a giant sunflower, she stops. Her eyes get as big as dinner plates.

There, sitting pretty as can be on a sunflower petal, is the most beautiful thing Safiya has ever seen—a butterfly! Its wings look like they're covered in tiny, sparkly jewels that dance in the sunlight. Safiya watches, totally amazed, as the butterfly moves from flower to flower. It's using its super-long nose (okay, it's called a proboscis, but who can say that?) to drink up the flower juice. Safiya can't believe her eyes. What a way to start the day!

The butterfly seemed to sense Safiya's presence and landed on a nearby leaf. "Hello, little one," it said in a gentle voice. "I see you are captivated by my beauty."

Safiya nodded shyly, still in awe of the butterfly's radiance. "You are the most beautiful creature I have ever seen!" she exclaimed. "How did you become so magnificent?"

The butterfly smiled and replied, "Dear, this beauty is not just a gift, but a reward for the journey I have taken. You see, I was once a caterpillar like you, crawling on the ground and munching on leaves."

Safiya's eyes widened with surprise. "You were a caterpillar? But how did you transform into this beautiful butterfly?"

The butterfly settled on the leaf and began to share its story. "This world, the garden we call home, is just a temporary place. It is a testing ground, where we must learn and grow, preparing ourselves for a greater life beyond."

Safiya listened intently, her curiosity piqued by the butterfly's words. "What do you mean by a greater life beyond?" she asked.

"My dear," the butterfly continued, "just as I transformed from a humble caterpillar into this beautiful creature, our souls will one day leave this world and experience a new life, an eternal life called the Hereafter."

Safiya had never heard of the Hereafter before, and she was eager to learn more. "The Hereafter?" she repeated, trying to wrap her tiny mind around the concept.

The butterfly nodded. "Yes, the Hereafter is the everlasting life that awaits us after our time in this world. It is a place of eternal bliss and reward for those who live righteously and follow the path of Allah, our Creator."

"And hasten towards forgiveness from your Lord and a Paradise as vast as the heavens and the earth, prepared for those mindful 'of Allah'. 'They are' those who donate in prosperity and adversity, control their anger, and pardon others. And Allah loves the good-doers."

[Surah Ali 'Imran, 3:133-134]

Safiya's eyes sparkled with wonder as she imagined a world beyond the garden, a place of endless beauty and joy. "How do we prepare for this Hereafter?" she asked.

"It is not an easy journey, my dear," the butterfly warned. "Just as I had to struggle and persevere through my transformation, we must strive to live a life of purpose, performing good deeds and seeking knowledge. We must not be consumed by the temporary pleasures of this world, but rather focus our efforts on pleasing Allah and earning His favor."

**The Prophet Muhammad (P.B.U.H) said:**

**"The Paradise is surrounded by hardships and the Hell-Fire is surrounded by temptations." [Sahih Muslim, 2822]**

As the butterfly shared its wisdom, Safiya noticed a group of caterpillars nearby, gorging themselves on the juiciest leaves and sweetest nectar. They seemed oblivious to the greater purpose the wise butterfly spoke of, consumed by the pleasures of the garden.

Safiya felt a sense of determination stirring within her. She knew that if she wanted to experience the beauty and eternal bliss of the Hereafter, she would need to seek guidance and understanding about her true purpose in life.

Safiya thanked the wise old butterfly for its words of wisdom. She promised herself that she would not be distracted by the temporary pleasures of the garden, but would instead focus on preparing for the ultimate journey that awaited her; the journey to the Hereafter.

As the sun set over the garden, Safiya felt a sense of excitement and anticipation. She had discovered a whole new world beyond the one she knew, and she couldn't wait to embark on the path that would lead her to the eternal rewards promised in the Hereafter.

# CHALLENGES IN THE GARDEN

After talking to the wise butterfly, Safiya felt different. It was like someone had flicked on a lightbulb inside her! She knew that she needed to prepare for the Hereafter, the eternal life that awaited her beyond the garden. But as she went along, she realized it wasn't going to be easy peasy.

The garden, which used to seem so perfect, was full of yummy distractions now! Everywhere Safiya crawled, there were delicious leaves and sweet nectar just begging her to gobble them up. It was hard to keep her mind on what really mattered!

Safiya found herself struggling to maintain the balance between fulfilling her worldly needs and preparing for her ultimate transformation. On one hand, she needed to eat and nourish her body, but on the other, she knew that she couldn't let herself become consumed by the temporary delights of the garden.

One day, Safiya was munching a juicy leaf when she heard a rustling sound nearby. WHOOSH! A bird swooped down from the sky, aiming its beak right at her. Safiya barely escaped! Her heart thumped like crazy. The garden wasn't just about yummy snacks, she realized. It was full of dangers and a place of trials and tests. The predators lurking around every corner reminded her of the challenges and obstacles that life in this world could present.

"And We will surely test you with something of fear and hunger and a loss of wealth and lives and fruits, but give good tidings to the patient."

[Surah Al-Baqarah, 2:155]

Despite the dangers, Safiya remained determined to stay on the path towards the Hereafter. She knew that these trials were part of her journey, and she needed to persevere with faith and resilience.

"Surely those who say, "Our Lord is Allah," and then remain steadfast—there will be no fear for them, nor will they grieve. It is they who will be the residents of Paradise, staying there forever, as a reward for what they used to do."

[Surah Al-Ahqaf, 46:13-14]

As she continued her journey, Safiya encountered other caterpillars who seemed to have forgotten the lessons of the wise butterfly. They spent their days gorging on the sweetest nectar, oblivious to the greater purpose that awaited them.

Safiya couldn't help but feel a sense of sadness for her fellow caterpillars. She wanted to share the wisdom she had learned and guide them toward the path of righteousness, but they seemed too consumed by the fleeting pleasures of the garden to listen.

Seeking guidance, Safiya sought out the elders of the garden; the wise old butterflies who had already completed their transformation.

These elders shared with her the importance of performing good deeds and living a righteous life in preparation for the Hereafter.

"My dear Safiya," one elder butterfly said, "the actions we take in this world will determine our eternal fate. Just as a caterpillar like you must spin its cocoon and undergo a transformation, we too must prepare our souls for the journey to the Hereafter."

Safiya listened intently, her determination to prepare for the Hereafter growing stronger with each word of wisdom she received. The elders taught her about the significance of good deeds, such as being kind to others, helping those in need, and seeking knowledge.

Despite the challenges and temptations that surrounded her, Safiya remained steadfast in her commitment to the path of righteousness. She knew that the temporary pleasures of the garden could never compare to the eternal bliss that awaited her in the Hereafter.

With each obstacle she overcame and each good deed she performed, Safiya's determination to prepare for the Hereafter grew stronger. She knew that the path ahead would not be easy, but with faith, perseverance, and a commitment to righteous living, she would one day experience the eternal rewards that awaited her in the everlasting life beyond the garden.

The Messenger of Allah (P.B.U.H) said:

"Whoever loves to meet Allah, Allah loves to meet him, and whoever hates to meet Allah, Allah hates to meet him."

[Sunan Ibn Majah: 4264]

# PREPARING FOR THE COCOON

As Safiya continued her journey through the garden, she could feel a change stirring within her. The wise words of the elders and the challenges she had overcome had prepared her for the next phase of her transformation; 'the cocoon'.

One morning, Safiya awoke to find herself feeling different as if a new energy was coursing through her tiny body. She looked around and noticed other caterpillars beginning to spin their cocoons, a sign that their time of transformation was near.

"What's happening?" Safiya asked one of the elder butterflies, her voice laced with a mixture of excitement and apprehension.

The elder butterfly landed gracefully on a nearby leaf and smiled. "My dear Safiya, you are about to embark on the most extraordinary journey of your life. The cocoon stage is a time of great transformation, where you will shed your caterpillar form and prepare for your new life as a butterfly."

Safiya's eyes widened with wonder, but she couldn't help but feel a twinge of fear. "Will it be difficult?" she asked, her voice trembling slightly.

The elder butterfly nodded. "The cocoon stage is not without its challenges, my dear. You will face inner struggles and doubts as you shed the limitations of your caterpillar existence and prepare for the new life that awaits you. These transformations are a part of our journey towards the Hereafter."

Safiya listened intently, her determination to face this new challenge growing stronger with each word. "Tell me more about the Hereafter," she said, eager to learn all she could.

The elder butterfly began to share the teachings of the wise ones, explaining the different stages of the Afterlife. "After our time in this world, we will face the Day of Judgement, where our actions and deeds will be weighed by Allah, the Most Merciful."

Safiya nodded, remembering the lessons she had learned about the importance of good deeds and righteous living.

"Those who have lived according to Allah's teachings and performed good deeds will be rewarded with eternal bliss in Paradise," the elder butterfly continued. "Paradise is a place of indescribable beauty and joy, where every desire will be fulfilled, and there will be no suffering or sadness."

Safiya's eyes sparkled with wonder as she tried to imagine such a place. "And what of those who strayed from the path?" she asked, her voice tinged with concern.

The elder butterfly's expression grew somber. "Those who turned away from Allah and lived in disregard for His teachings will face punishment in Hell, a place of torment and suffering."

**The Messenger of Allah (P.B.U.H) said:**

"Paradise and the Fire (Hell) were shown to me, and I have never seen a better thing than Paradise, or a worse thing than the Fire." [Sahih Al-Bukhari]

Safiya shuddered at the thought of the Hellfire.

As the days went by, Safiya started to spin her own cocoon, an intricate web of silk that would keep her safe during her transformation. While she worked, she felt a sense of inner turmoil, her mind swirling with doubts and questions about the journey ahead.

"What if I'm not ready?" she thought to herself.

In her moments of doubt, Safiya would seek guidance from the elders, who reminded her of the importance of patience and trust in Allah's plan.

"My dear Safiya," one elder butterfly said gently, "the journey ahead may seem daunting, but remember that Allah has prepared this path for you. Have faith in His wisdom and mercy, and trust that He will guide you through this transformation."

Safiya nodded.

As her cocoon took shape, Safiya began to experience glimpses of the Hereafter, visions of the rewards and punishments that awaited her based on her actions in this life. She saw the breathtaking beauty of Paradise, with its lush gardens, flowing rivers, and eternal peace. But she also witnessed the horrors of Hell, a place of fire and torment, where the wrongdoers would suffer for eternity.

These visions served as powerful reminders for Safiya, motivating her to remain steadfast in her faith and commitment to good deeds. She knew that the choices she made in this life would determine her eternal fate, and she was determined to earn the rewards of Paradise.

Through it all, Safiya's mentors—the wise elder butterflies—guided her with patience and compassion. They shared stories of their own transformations, offering words of encouragement and wisdom to help Safiya navigate the challenges she faced.

"Remember, my dear," one elder butterfly said, "the cocoon is not a prison, but a space where you prepare for your new life. Embrace this time of transformation, and trust in Allah's plan for you."

## SAFIYA's TRANSFORMATION

Weeks flew by, and Safiya could feel herself changing inside her cocoon. It was like her caterpillar self was molting away, and a brand-new Safiya was getting ready to burst out! She knew it was almost time to leave the cocoon, and she felt both excited and nervous, all at the same time.

Finally, the big day arrived! Safiya pushed her way out of the cocoon and blinked in the bright sunshine. Stretching her brand-new wings, she looked around. The garden seemed totally different! The colors were brighter, everything had new textures, and Safiya felt amazing! She was a beautiful butterfly now, ready for an amazing new life!

She flapped her new wings gently and gasped. They were covered in the prettiest patterns, sparkling in the sun like magic glitter.

As Safiya looked around her old garden home with her new butterfly eyes, she felt like she was in a dream. But it was real! She wasn't a little caterpillar anymore. She was ready for all the awesome adventures waiting for her in the garden to come.

Safiya spread her wings and soared into the air, ready for a brand-new adventure!

"Wow!" she whispered. Her voice even sounded different now, kind of musical.

For the first time ever, Safiya felt totally free. No more crawling around like when she was a caterpillar! Now she was a butterfly, floating from one flower to the next, sipping nectar.

A warm, happy feeling spread through Safiya's heart. She had made it through the tough times inside the cocoon, and now look! She was surrounded by beauty and freedom. Anything felt possible!

Up ahead, Safiya saw a group of butterflies. Their wings were so colorful, with fancy designs! Excited, she fluttered over to meet them. These butterflies had gone through the same kind of change she had!

"Welcome, sister!" said one of the butterflies. "We were waiting for you."

As Safiya looked around at the other butterflies, she felt like she belonged. They all had different colors and markings, each one special in its own way! But they'd all become butterflies together.

"This is amazing!" Safiya whispered. She had never imagined anything so wonderful.

The butterflies nodded in agreement, their delicate antennae swaying gently. "This is but a glimpse of the eternal bliss that awaits us in the Hereafter," one of them explained. "Just as we have shed our caterpillar forms and emerged as beautiful creatures, our souls will one day leave behind the temporary confines of this world and enter into the everlasting realm of Paradise."

"Indeed, those who believe and do good will have the Gardens of Paradise as an accommodation, where they will be forever, never desiring anywhere else."

[Surah Al-Kahf, 18:107-108]

Safiya listened closely, her heart buzzing with excitement. The butterflies were telling her all about the Hereafter. It all came back to her now: the lessons she'd learned in the cocoon about living a good life and doing kind things. That's how you earn a spot in Paradise!

"Tell me more about Paradise," Safiya pleaded, her wings fluttering.

The butterflies took turns describing it. They painted a picture in her mind: lush gardens, sparkly rivers, and houses decorated with jewels! It was a place without sadness, pain, or fear. Only never-ending happiness!

"The best part," added one butterfly, "is that you get to be close to Allah, the Most Merciful, and feel his love forever."

Safiya felt a wave of awe. Paradise sounded almost too good to be true! But deep down, she knew it was real. If you believed and did the right things, you could reach it.

She remembered what the elders had taught her about good deeds and getting ready for the Hereafter. Back in the cocoon, Safiya had felt unsure, wondering if she was ready to change. But her faith in Allah had made her strong.

Now, surrounded by all the butterflies, Safiya felt grateful. She had stayed on the right path, and look where it led! She was living proof that doing the right thing brought amazing rewards.

"I am so thankful," she said, her voice filled with emotion. "Thankful for the lessons I learned, the challenges I overcame, and the guidance I received along the way. Without them, I might never have been prepared for this incredible journey."

The butterflies nodded in agreement, their wings fluttering in a gentle rhythm. "We all have our own stories, our own struggles and triumphs," one of them said. "But in the end, it will be our faith in Allah and our commitment to living according to His teachings that will get us to the place of eternal bliss."

Safiya pondered for a moment.

"I will tell my story," she promised herself. "I will share the lessons I have learned with all those who will listen. For it is through this wisdom that we can all find our way to the eternal rewards of Paradise."

**"Those who believe and do good will be admitted into Gardens, under which rivers flow—to stay there forever by the Will of their Lord—where they will be greeted with 'Peace!'"**

**[Surah Ibrahim, 14:23]**

## SHARING THE WISDOM

As Safiya flitted through the garden, she met lots of caterpillars. They seemed lost, totally focused on gobbling snacks and lazing around. They didn't seem to know about the amazing journey that was waiting for them!

With a kind smile, Safiya would fly over to say hello. "Hi there!" she'd say in her musical voice. "I used to be just like you, happy to hang out in the garden. I didn't know anything about the amazing journey that was waiting for me!"

The caterpillars would stare, their little eyes wide with curiosity. Safiya's colorful wings and beautiful colors grabbed their attention.

"But then I learned about the eternal life that awaits us," Safiya would explain. "It's the life that comes after this one, and it lasts forever! Our time in this garden is like a test. What we do here decides whether we get incredible rewards... or punishments... in the next life."

As she spoke, Safiya could see the caterpillars becoming captivated by her words, their eyes widening with wonder and curiosity. Some would ask questions, yearning to learn more about this concept of the Hereafter and the path that led to it.

"Remember, my friends," she would say, "the pleasures of this worldly life are temporary and fleeting. While it is important to nourish your bodies and enjoy the beauty around you, you must also dedicate time and effort to nourishing your souls and preparing for the everlasting life that awaits you.

The actions we take in this life will have an eternal impact. Every good deed we perform, every act of kindness and righteousness, will be rewarded in the Hereafter. And every transgression, every selfish act or disregard for Allah's teachings, will be accounted for on the Day of Judgment."

"Whoever does good, whether male or female, and is a believer, We will surely bless them with a good life, and We will certainly reward them according to the best of their deeds."

[Surah An-Nahl, 16:97]

Safiya's teachings resonated with many of the caterpillars, inspiring them to embrace the concept of the Hereafter and to live a life of purpose. They began to seek out the wisdom of the elders and to perform good deeds, such as helping those in need, being kind to their fellow caterpillars, and seeking knowledge.

As word of Safiya's teachings spread, more and more caterpillars flocked to her, eager to learn about the path to the Hereafter. Safiya welcomed them all with open wings, sharing her story and the lessons she had learned with unwavering patience and compassion.

Her teachings spread throughout the garden and beyond. Anyone who heard Safiya's tale remembered how important it was to live a good life because this life was just the beginning!

**The Messenger of Allah (P.B.U.H) said:**

**"The likeness of the person who remembers Allah and the one who does not remember Allah is like the living and the dead." [Sahih Al-Bukhari: 6407]**

# FRIENDS FIGHTING SHAYTAAN'S WHISPERS!

An Islamic Story on Understanding the Concept of Shaytaan

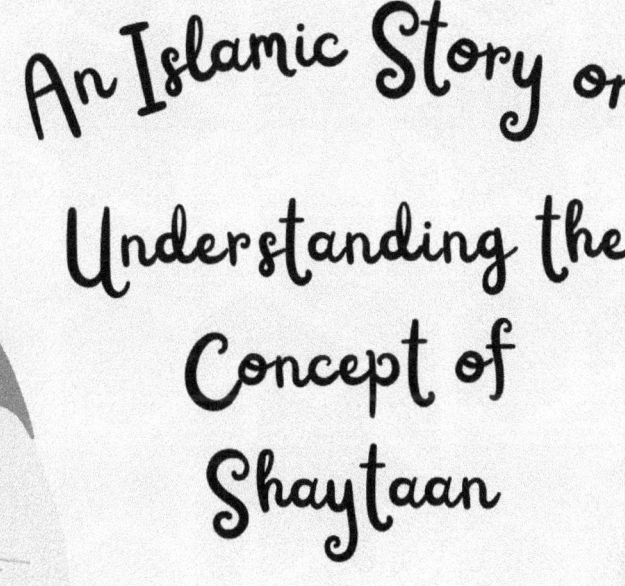

# OMAR's BIG IDEA

The sun peeked through the curtains, painting stripes of light on Omar's bedroom floor. He yawned and stretched, still feeling a bit tired even though it was morning. He knew he had stayed up way too late playing video games again.

"Omar! Time for school!" his mom called from downstairs.

Omar sighed. He loved playing games, but sometimes it was hard to stop. He knew he should be spending more time on his studies, but the games were just so exciting!

At school, Omar met up with his friends: Sarah, Ali, Fatima, and Hassan. They were all in the same class and loved playing together during recess.

Sarah had a big smile, but she looked a little tired, too. She confessed to Omar, "I ate too many sweets last night. My tummy hurts, and I don't have the energy to play tag today."

Ali slumped down on a bench, already out of breath. "I wish I had exercised more," he said. "Running is so hard!"

Fatima watched another girl showing off her new sparkly shoes. A frown crossed Fatima's face. "I wish I had those shoes," she mumbled to herself.

Hassan, always wanting to be cool, noticed a group of older boys wearing the same style of cap. He tugged at his own plain cap, wishing he had one like theirs.

Omar looked at his friends, each with their own little struggles. He had an idea!

"Hey guys," he said, "I have a suggestion. Let's start a club!"

"A club?" Sarah asked. "What kind of club?"

"We can call it 'The Conscience Club'," Omar explained. "We can help each other be better people and do the things we know we should be doing. You know, like how our Prophet Muhammad (P.B.U.H) always encouraged us to be our best selves and help others."

"Like what?" Ali asked, still catching his breath.

"Like, I can help you exercise more," Omar said to Ali, "and you can help me stop playing video games so much."

"And I can help you eat healthier snacks," Sarah said to Omar, "if you remind me not to eat too many sweets."

Fatima and Hassan nodded, agreeing that they could all use some support to overcome their weaknesses.

Omar's eyes sparkled with excitement. "We can even have a motto!" he exclaimed.

"What's a motto?" little Hassan asked.

"It's like a special saying that reminds us what our club is all about," Omar explained.

They all thought for a moment. Then Fatima said, "How about 'Listen to your heart, do what's right, and be the best you can be!'"

Everyone loved it! They decided to meet every week after school to discuss their goals and help each other stay on track.

In addition, they sought Allah's guidance to stay devoted to their club goals.

Little did they know that a sneaky and sly creature was watching them from afar. It was Shaytaan, the enemy of all good things. He saw how these friends wanted to improve themselves and become closer to Allah. He didn't like that one bit.

"Oh no, you don't," Shaytaan muttered to himself. "I won't let you become good and strong. I will whisper bad thoughts into your ears and make you forget your promises."

\*\*\*

The next day, as Omar walked home from school, he passed by a video game store. The latest game was displayed in the window, with bright colors and exciting characters.

"Just one game," Shaytaan whispered in Omar's ear. "You deserve a little fun after school."

Omar hesitated. He remembered his promise to the Conscience Club, but the game looked so tempting. He decided to just take a peek inside the store...

Meanwhile, Sarah was walking home with her mom when they passed by a bakery. The sweet smell of freshly baked cookies filled the air.

"Mommy, can I please have a cookie?" Sarah asked.

"Remember what we talked about, honey," her mom said gently. "Too much sugar is not good for you. How about we have some fruit when we get home?"

Shaytaan seized the opportunity. "Just one cookie won't hurt," he whispered to Sarah. "It looks so delicious, and you've been so good lately."

Sarah looked at the cookies with longing. Her mom was busy looking at her phone. Maybe just one small bite...

And so, each friend faced their first challenge, unaware that Shaytaan was playing tricks on their minds. Would they be able to resist his whispers and stay true to their promises? The Conscience Club had just begun, and the journey ahead would be full of tests and triumphs.

# SHAYTAAN's WHISPERS

Days turned into weeks, and the initial excitement of The Conscience Club began to fade. Shaytaan, never giving up, continued whispering doubts and temptations into each friend's mind. He knew their weaknesses and used them against them, like a sneaky spider spinning a web.

Omar found it harder and harder to resist the lure of video games. The newest adventure game had him hooked, and he spent hours exploring virtual worlds and battling imaginary monsters. The colorful graphics and exciting challenges made him forget about everything else, even his five daily prayers.

"Just one more level," Shaytaan would whisper. "You can pray later. Allah is merciful, He will understand."

Omar knew he was making excuses, but Shaytaan's words were like a sweet poison, slowly numbing his conscience. He started skipping afternoon prayers, telling himself he was too tired or would make it up later. But "later" never seemed to come.

Sarah, despite her good intentions, struggled with her sweet tooth. Shaytaan tempted her with sugary treats at every turn; candies at the supermarket checkout, ice cream trucks with their cheerful jingles, and classmates sharing birthday cupcakes.

"One little treat won't hurt," Shaytaan would whisper. "You deserve a reward for being so good."

Sarah tried to resist, but the cravings were strong. She started sneaking sweets when her mom wasn't looking, feeling guilty but unable to stop. Soon, she started feeling sluggish and tired all the time. Her clothes felt tighter, and she didn't have the energy to play with her friends like she used to.

Ali, known for his relaxed attitude, became even lazier. Shaytaan convinced him that doing chores and homework was boring and unnecessary.

"Take a nap instead," Shaytaan would whisper. "You can do it later. Relax, there's no rush."

Ali found himself procrastinating more and more. His room became messy, his schoolwork piled up, and his parents were disappointed in his lack of responsibility. He knew he should be doing better, but Shaytaan's voice made him feel like it was okay to just lie down and do nothing.

Fatima's envy grew like a weed in her heart. Shaytaan fueled her jealousy, pointing out all the things others had that she didn't: nicer clothes, better toys, higher grades.

"It's not fair," Shaytaan would whisper. "Why do they have so much while you have so little? You deserve better."

Fatima started comparing herself to everyone, feeling resentful and unhappy. She lost sight of her own blessings and forgot the importance of being grateful for what she had. Instead of being happy for her friends' successes, she felt a pang of jealousy every time they achieved something.

Hassan, always wanting to fit in, became obsessed with following the latest trends. Shaytaan whispered doubts about his own identity and convinced him that he needed to be like everyone else to be accepted.

"Everyone is doing it," Shaytaan would whisper. "You don't want to be left out, do you? Be cool, be trendy, be like them."

Hassan started wearing clothes he didn't like, listening to music he didn't enjoy, and even saying things he didn't believe in, just to feel like he belonged. He started neglecting his prayers and Islamic values, thinking they were outdated and uncool.

As the weeks passed, The Conscience Club meetings became less frequent. The friends were too ashamed to admit their struggles, and Shaytaan's whispers kept them isolated and discouraged. They felt guilty and frustrated with themselves, but they didn't know how to break free from the web of temptation.

Omar's room was a mess of empty snack wrappers and soda cans. He barely slept, his eyes red and tired from staring at the screen. He missed spending time with his family and felt a growing emptiness inside.

Sarah's once bright smile had dimmed. She felt sluggish and unhappy with her appearance. She avoided looking in the mirror and started withdrawing from her friends, ashamed of her eating habits.

Ali's laziness affected every aspect of his life. He received failing grades, his room was a disaster zone, and his parents were constantly disappointed in him. He felt trapped in a cycle of procrastination and guilt.

Fatima's envy poisoned her relationships. She became withdrawn and irritable, finding fault with everyone and everything. She lost the joy and appreciation for the good things in her life, focusing only on what she lacked.

Hassan felt lost and confused. He tried so hard to fit in, but he never truly felt like he belonged. His attempts to be cool only made him feel more like a fake, and he was losing sight of his own values and identity.

The once close-knit group of friends drifted apart, each struggling alone in the darkness of Shaytaan's web. They had fallen into temptation, forgetting the promises they made to each other and the importance of listening to their conscience. Their hearts felt heavy, their spirits low, and their connection to Allah grew weaker with every passing day.

"Satan only makes them 'false' promises and deludes them with 'empty' hopes. Truly Satan promises them nothing but delusion."

[Surah An-Nisa: 4:120]

# WAKE-UP CALLS!

One night, as Omar drifted off to sleep after another long gaming session, he had a strange dream. He found himself in a beautiful garden, filled with fragrant flowers and the sound of birdsong. An old man with a long white beard and kind eyes sat under a shady tree, reading a book.

Omar approached the old man, feeling a sense of peace and curiosity. "Excuse me, sir," he said politely. "Who are you?"

The old man smiled warmly. "I am a friend," he replied. "And who might you be, young man?"

"I am Omar," he answered.

"Ah, Omar," the old man said, his eyes twinkling. "I know why you are here."

Omar was surprised. "You do?"

The old man nodded. "You are lost in a world of illusions, a world that steals your time, your energy, and your connection to Allah."

Omar felt a pang of guilt. He knew the old man was talking about his video game addiction.

"But the games are so much fun," Omar protested. "They help me relax and escape from my problems."

The old man chuckled softly. "True enjoyment comes from living a life that pleases Allah," he explained. "Remember, Omar, you were created for a greater purpose than just playing games. You have a mind to learn, a heart to love, and a soul to connect with your Creator."

Omar woke up feeling shaken and confused. The old man's words echoed in his mind, making him question his choices. He looked at his messy room, the pile of unfinished homework, and the neglected Quran on his shelf. He felt super embarrassed.

Meanwhile, Sarah had a surprising encounter of her own. While walking home from school, feeling tired and bloated from too many sweets, she met a friendly woman with a bright smile and a basket full of fresh fruits and vegetables.

The woman introduced herself as a nutritionist and noticed Sarah's lack of energy. She explained the importance of healthy eating habits and how sugary treats can affect our bodies and minds.

"Fruits and vegetables are like fuel for your body," she explained. "They give you energy to play, learn, and grow. Too much sugar can make you feel tired and sluggish, just like a car running on the wrong kind of fuel."

Sarah listened intently, realizing how her unhealthy eating habits were affecting her. The nutritionist gave her some tips on making healthy choices and encouraged her to try new fruits and vegetables.

Ali's wake-up call came in the form of a visit from his older cousin, Ahmed. Ahmed was known for his discipline and hard work. He excelled in school, played sports, and always helped his family.

Seeing Ali lounging on the couch, Ahmed raised an eyebrow. "Shouldn't you be doing your homework?" he asked.

Ali mumbled something about doing it later. Ahmed sat down next to him and shared a story about the Prophet Muhammad (P.B.U.H) and his emphasis on hard work and productivity.

"The Prophet (P.B.U.H) said, 'The best of people are those who benefit others.' [Al-Mu'jam Al-Awsaṭ 5937]" Ahmed explained. "By being lazy, you are not only harming yourself but also missing out on the opportunity to help others and contribute to the world."

Ali felt a spark of inspiration. He realized that his laziness wasn't just about him; it was affecting his family and his ability to be a good Muslim.

Fatima's encounter was a lesson in gratitude and contentment. While walking through the park, feeling envious of a girl with a new bicycle, she met an elderly woman sitting on a bench, feeding pigeons.

The woman noticed Fatima's sad expression and asked what was wrong. Fatima confessed her feelings of envy, wishing she had a bicycle like the other girl.

The old woman smiled gently. "My dear," she said, "true happiness comes not from what we have, but from being grateful for what Allah has given us. Look around you; the sunshine, the birds singing, the fresh air we breathe, a bicycle to ride; these are all blessings from Allah. Think about people who are less fortunate than you."

Fatima looked around and realized the truth in the old woman's words. She had been so focused on what she lacked that she had forgotten to appreciate all the good things in her life.

Hassan's dream was a powerful reminder of his own identity. He found himself in a vast library, surrounded by books filled with knowledge. A wise scholar with a long beard and a warm smile approached him.

"Young man," the scholar said, "why do you follow the crowd without questioning? Allah has given you a mind to think and a heart to understand. Do not blindly imitate others, for the path to truth lies in seeking knowledge and following the guidance of Allah."

Hassan woke up, feeling both confused and inspired. The scholar's words reminded him of the importance of his faith and the need to make his own choices based on Islamic principles. He realized that following trends blindly was leading him away from his true self and from Allah.

"If Allah helps you none shall prevail over you; if He forsakes you then who can help you? It is in Allah that the believers should put their trust."

[Surah Ali 'Imran: 3:160]

# UNMASKING THE ENEMY

The next day at school, the friends couldn't stop thinking about their dreams and encounters. They felt a sense of urgency to share their experiences with each other.

During recess, they gathered under their favorite shady tree, the same place where they had formed The Conscience Club weeks ago.

"My dream was so strange," Omar began, his voice filled with wonder. "I met this wise old man who told me I was wasting my time with video games."

"That's funny," Sarah chimed in. "I met a lady who told me I should eat more fruits and vegetables instead of sweets."

One by one, each friend shared their experiences, the details of their dreams and encounters weaving together like pieces of a puzzle.

"Wait a minute," Ali exclaimed, his eyes widening. "Do you think these were just regular dreams, or maybe... something more?"

Fatima gasped. "Maybe it was Allah's help!"

Hassan nodded excitedly. "Yeah! Like a secret message to be steadfast in our faith!"

They started piecing together the clues. The wise old man, the nutritionist, the productive cousin, the compassionate woman, and the learned scholar—they were all like guides sent by Allah, showing them the right path.

"But who was trying to lead us astray?" Omar wondered aloud.

They thought back to all the times they had given in to temptation; the whispers that told them to play more games, eat more sweets, be lazy, feel envious, and follow the crowd.

Suddenly, it all clicked. They remembered learning about Shaytaan in their Islamic studies class. He was the one who whispered bad thoughts and tried to lead people away from Allah.

"It was Shaytaan!" Hassan exclaimed. "He was the one trying to trick us!"

"Surely Satan is an enemy to you, so take him as an enemy. He only invites his followers to become inmates of the Blaze."

[Surah Fatir, 35:6]

A shiver ran down their spines as they realized the true enemy they were facing. Shaytaan, the deceiver, had been playing games with their minds, making them forget their goals and neglect their faith.

Omar felt a surge of anger towards Shaytaan for making him waste so much time and neglect his prayers. Sarah felt remorse for ignoring her health and giving in to her sweet tooth. Ali was ashamed of his laziness and the disappointment he had caused his parents. Fatima regretted her envy and the negativity it brought into her life. Hassan felt foolish for blindly following trends and compromising his values.

They realized that The Conscience Club wasn't just about self-improvement; it was a battle against Shaytaan. They needed to be stronger, more knowledgeable, and more united than ever before.

With renewed determination, they decided to learn more about Shaytaan's tactics and how to resist his influence. They borrowed books from the library, talked to their parents and teachers, and even searched for information online.

They learned that Shaytaan was cunning and persistent, using different tricks on different people. He would whisper doubts, magnify desires, and make wrong things seem appealing. He would even use their friends, family, and the media to lead them astray.

But they also learned that Shaytaan was weak and powerless against those who had strong faith and relied on Allah's protection. The Quran and the teachings of Prophet Muhammad (P.B.U.H) provided them with a clear roadmap for resisting Shaytaan's whispers and staying on the right path.

> "If you are tempted by Satan, then seek refuge with Allah. Surely He is All-Hearing, All-Knowing. Indeed, when Satan whispers to those mindful 'of Allah', they remember 'their Lord' then they start to see 'things' clearly."
>
> [Surah Al-A'raf, 7:200-201]

They decided to resume their Conscience Club meetings with a renewed focus. They set new goals based on Islamic principles:

Omar: To prioritize his prayers and limit his video game time.

Sarah: To make healthy eating choices and focus on nourishing her body and mind.

Ali: To overcome his laziness and fulfill his responsibilities with dedication.

Fatima: To practice gratitude and appreciate her blessings instead of envying others.

Hassan: To develop his own identity based on Islamic values and resist the pressure to blindly follow trends.

They created a chart to track their progress and promised to support each other through every challenge. They knew that the journey ahead wouldn't be easy, but they were determined to fight back against Shaytaan and become the best versions of themselves, with Allah's help and the support of their true friends.

# STRONGER TOGETHER

The members of The Conscience Club embarked on their journey of self-improvement with renewed determination. They faced challenges along the way, but they had each other's backs, like a team of superheroes fighting against a common enemy; 'Shaytaan'.

Omar still felt the pull of video games, especially when his friends talked about the latest releases. But now, he had strategies in place. He set time limits for gaming, prayed on time, and engaged in other activities he enjoyed, like reading Islamic stories and playing soccer with his friends. Whenever he felt tempted, he would remember the wise old man from his dream and the purpose he was striving for.

Sarah still craved sweets sometimes, but she made healthier choices most of the time. She started packing fruits and vegetables for snacks, discovered delicious healthy recipes with her mom, and even joined a sports team to stay active. The sluggishness and tiredness disappeared, replaced by energy and a newfound confidence.

Ali struggled with his habit of procrastination, but he found that breaking down tasks into smaller steps made them less daunting. He set alarms to remind himself of deadlines, created a schedule for his chores and homework, and even started waking up earlier to pray Fajr with his dad. He felt a sense of accomplishment with each completed task and discovered that being productive was actually rewarding.

Fatima still noticed things that others had and she didn't, but she learned to shift her focus. She started a gratitude journal, writing down things she was thankful for each day. She realized how blessed she was with a loving family, good friends, and countless other gifts from Allah. She also made a conscious effort to celebrate her friends' achievements, replacing envy with genuine happiness for their success.

Hassan still saw others following trends, but he no longer felt the pressure to conform. He learned about the importance of being true to himself and his values. He embraced his identity as a Muslim and started making choices based on what he believed was right, even if it meant being different from the crowd. He rediscovered the joy of learning about Islam and felt a sense of peace knowing he was on the right path.

The Conscience Club meetings became a source of strength and encouragement for everyone. They shared their progress, celebrated each other's successes, and offered support whenever someone stumbled. They learned from each other's experiences and discovered the power of unity in their fight against Shaytaan.

"I almost gave in to playing video games all day yesterday," Omar confessed during one meeting. "But then I remembered what the old man in my dream said, and I decided to go for a walk with my family instead."

"That's amazing, Omar!" Sarah exclaimed. "It's not easy to resist temptation, but you did it!"

"And guess what?" Ali chimed in. "I finished all my homework on time this week! No more procrastination for me!"

Fatima smiled. "I saw a girl with a beautiful new dress today, and instead of feeling envious, I was happy for her and prayed that Allah would bless her."

Hassan added, "I told my friends that I don't want to listen to music with bad words anymore, and they respected my decision."

The friends realized that their individual struggles were not unique. Other children were facing similar challenges with temptation, distraction, and peer pressure. They decided to share their experiences and knowledge with others, hoping to inspire them to resist Shaytaan's influence and develop their own strong conscience.

They organized group meetings at their school and local mosque, sharing stories, creating artwork, and performing skits about the importance of listening to one's conscience and making good choices. They even joined their mosque's mentorship program, pairing up with the Imam to offer guidance and support to younger children.

The Conscience Club became a beacon of positivity in the community, inspiring others to form similar groups and create a network of support against Shaytaan's deceptions. Parents and teachers praised their efforts, recognizing the positive impact they were having on the children's character and spiritual development.

The friends knew that staying on the right path wouldn't be easy, and that Shaytaan would always try to lead them astray. But they felt strong and confident because they had each other, and they had a powerful guidebook - the Quran - to show them the way. They also had the example of the Prophet Muhammad (P.B.U.H) to inspire them, and their own conscience to remind them of what is right and wrong. Most importantly, they had faith in Allah, who would always be with them and help them through tough times.

As the day came to a close, the sun dipped low in the sky, stretching long shadows across the playground. Under their favorite tree, the friends from The Conscience Club gathered together, their faces beaming with thankfulness and excitement. They looked at each other, eager to share and support one another, and ready to make a difference.

"Remember," Omar said, "Shaytaan will never stop trying to trick us. But we are stronger than him, especially when we are united."

"And we have the Quran and Ahadees to guide us," Sarah added. "It's like a compass that always points us in the right direction."

Ali smiled. "And we have each other," he said. "Together, we can overcome any obstacle and achieve anything we set our minds to."

They raised their hands together, their voices ringing out in unison: "Listen to your heart, do what's right, and be the best you can be!"

The Messenger of Allah (P.B.U.H) said:

"A believer is like a brick for another believer, the one supporting the other."

[Sahih Muslim 2585]

# IBRAHIM LEARNS THE POWER OF DUA

An Islamic Story on

Understanding the Meaning of Dua

# UNCLE FAROOQ's GARDEN

Ibrahim woke to the sound of cheerful birds singing outside his window. Sunshine poured through the curtains, painting his room gold. It was going to be a good day—a super special day, actually! Today, Ibrahim was going to visit his Uncle Farooq!

Just thinking about Uncle Farooq made Ibrahim grin. His uncle was full of wisdom and the best stories! Every visit was an adventure.

Ibrahim got dressed as fast as a firefighter puts on his gear. He could barely contain his excitement! Downstairs, the most delicious smell greeted him; Mom had made fresh bread and sweet tea.

"Good morning, my little explorer," Mom said, giving him a hug and ruffling his hair.

"Mmm, it smells amazing!" Ibrahim said, giving her a big kiss on the cheek.

At the breakfast table, Dad winked at him. "Ready for your journey today?"

Ibrahim nodded enthusiastically. "Yes! I wonder what stories Uncle Farooq will tell this time!"

After gobbling up his breakfast, Ibrahim tugged on Dad's hand. "Can we go now? Pleeeease?"

Dad chuckled and patted his head. "Hold your horses, son. Good things come to those who wait."

That was easy for Dad to say! To Ibrahim, it felt like the longest wait ever before they finally set off on their adventure.

The city streets were a whirlwind of activity! Cars honked, people chatted, and vendors called out, trying to sell their wares. The air buzzed with a jumble of sounds and the tempting aromas of street food: spicy kababs, sweet baklava, freshly baked bread...

Ibrahim's eyes darted back and forth, trying to take it all in. Finally, they reached Uncle Farooq's cozy little house, tucked away on a quiet street. Ibrahim jumped out of the car and raced up to the front door, practically bouncing with excitement. He knocked as loudly as he could.

The door swung open, revealing Uncle Farooq's warm smile. "Ah, my dear Ibrahim! You're just in time!"

Ibrahim threw his arms around his uncle. "Assalamu alaikum, Uncle!"

"Wa alaikum assalam, Ibrahim!" Uncle Farooq said, hugging him back. "Come, let's go to the garden."

Ibrahim's parents bid farewell to Uncle Farooq from the car and indicated that they would return shortly after running some errands.

Hand-in-hand, they walked through the house and into the prettiest garden Ibrahim had ever seen. Flowers of every color imaginable bloomed in neat rows, their sweet perfume carried on the gentle breeze. Butterflies flitted from petal to petal, their wings like stained glass in the sunshine.

Uncle Farooq and Ibrahim settled onto comfy cushions under the shade of a gnarled, ancient olive tree. It felt like a secret world, hidden away from the busyness of the city.

"Now then, young friend," Uncle Farooq said, stroking his beard. "What shall we talk about today?"

Ibrahim scrunched up his face, thinking hard. "I've been wondering about dua lately," he said finally.

Uncle Farooq nodded thoughtfully, stroking his long beard. "Ah yes, the blessed path of talking to Allah. A very important thing indeed."

"Dad says dua is how we speak to Allah," Ibrahim said in a small voice. "But sometimes...I'm not sure if He hears me."

Uncle Farooq looked at Ibrahim with kind, serious eyes. "Dear boy, dua is more than just words. It's a way to connect our hearts to Allah's never-ending wisdom."

Ibrahim's eyes widened, hanging onto his uncle's every word.

"When we make dua, we open our hearts to Allah," Uncle Farooq continued gently. "The true purpose is to grow closer to Him, not just to get what we ask for."

Ibrahim thought hard about this. It was a new way of thinking about dua.

After a quiet moment, Ibrahim spoke again. "I want to really understand dua, Uncle. Will you teach me more?"

Uncle Farooq smiled, his eyes twinkling. "Of course, my dear. Let's start with the saying of the Messenger of Allah, peace be upon him. He said that Dua is the essence of worship. It is the weapon of the weak and suppressed."

"Think about that, Ibrahim," Uncle Farooq said. "The prophets and righteous people knew how powerful dua was. It helped them stay strong, even during the most difficult times."

Ibrahim leaned forward, his brow furrowed. "But Uncle, why doesn't Allah answer all our prayers right away? Doesn't He hear us?"

Uncle Farooq chuckled softly. "An excellent question, and one that many people have pondered. You must understand, my dear boy, Allah's wisdom and plans are far beyond what we can possibly grasp."

Ibrahim frowned, turning this over in his mind.

"When we make dua, we ask for what we think we want in that moment," Uncle Farooq explained patiently. "But Allah, the Lord of the Worlds, knows what is truly best for us, even if it's different from what we asked for."

He placed a comforting hand on Ibrahim's shoulder. "Having our prayers answered exactly as we ask is not the true purpose of dua, Ibrahim. The greatest blessing lies in turning our hearts to our Merciful Creator."

A feeling of understanding bloomed inside Ibrahim, like one of the flowers in his uncle's garden. Uncle Farooq's words felt true, deep down.

"Sometimes," Uncle Farooq continued, "our prayers are answered in ways we don't expect. But those answers might lead us to something even better—like when raindrops fall on a tiny seed and help it grow into a beautiful flower."

Ibrahim nodded slowly. He could picture that! Flowers needed time and care to bloom.

"The most important thing, my dear nephew, is to make dua with your whole heart. Believe in Allah, and trust that His timing is perfect."

A smile spread across Ibrahim's face. "I think I understand now, Uncle. Thank you."

Uncle Farooq beamed, squeezing Ibrahim's hand. "You have a good heart, Ibrahim, one that seeks knowledge. If you stay on this path, Allah's mercy will surely be revealed to you."

Uncle Farooq's words had left a lasting impression of wisdom in Ibrahim's heart. He knew he had so much more to learn about dua and he couldn't wait to learn more!

# WHEN PRAYERS FEEL UNANSWERED

Over the next few weeks, Ibrahim held onto Uncle Farooq's words like a compass, guiding him on the path of dua. Every night, he prayed with his whole heart, his voice full of sincerity.

"O Allah," he'd whisper, "help me to be patient and trust in Your plan, just like the Prophets did..."

Closing his eyes, Ibrahim would lose himself in the rhythm of his prayers, a feeling of peace washing over him. He felt closer to Allah than ever before.

But then, dark clouds gathered on the horizon, threatening to test everything Ibrahim thought he'd learned.

One morning, Ibrahim ran downstairs, ready for breakfast and fun. But when he saw his parents, his smile vanished. Their faces were drawn, and a heavy silence filled the air.

"What's wrong?" Ibrahim asked, his heart starting to thump.

Mom pulled him into a tight hug. "It's Uncle Farooq..." she began, her voice trembling. "He's very sick."

The words hit Ibrahim like a punch in the gut. His wise, strong Uncle Farooq... sick? It couldn't be true!

The next few days were a blur of worry. Ibrahim prayed harder than he'd ever prayed before, begging Allah to heal his beloved uncle.

"Please, O Allah, please!" he cried, tears streaming down his face. "Not Uncle Farooq! I'll do anything, just please make him better!"

But time marched on, and Uncle Farooq only grew weaker. Ibrahim's hopeful prayers seemed to vanish into thin air, unanswered.

Confusion and doubt gnawed at his heart. Hadn't Uncle Farooq taught him that Allah always listens to sincere supplications? So why was this happening?

A quiet anger, a feeling Ibrahim had rarely known before, started to burn inside him. His faith, so strong just days ago, felt shaky.

One night, he went outside and looked up at the vast, star-studded sky. "Why won't You listen?" he shouted, his voice cracking. "I'm doing everything right! Why are You ignoring me?"

But the stars just twinkled silently, and Ibrahim's anger turned into tears.

Ibrahim's parents saw how much he was struggling, and they knew they had to help before doubt took over completely.

One evening, as Ibrahim trudged to his room, his shoulders slumped, Dad stopped him. "Son," he said gently, "we need to talk."

Ibrahim shrugged, his eyes downcast. "What's the point? My prayers aren't working anyway."

Dad was worried about what Ibrahim was going through. He sat down on the edge of Ibrahim's bed. "Do you remember the story of

Prophet Ayyub (P.B.U.H)?" he asked. "The one Uncle Farooq told you? About all the hardships he endured without ever losing faith?"

Ibrahim thought back to the story. He nodded slowly, remembering.

"For a long, long time, it seemed like Prophet Ayyub's prayers went unanswered," Dad continued. "Terrible things kept happening. But through it all, he never stopped believing in Allah's plan."

Dad's voice softened. "The Quran reminds us that Allah is always near, always listening:

'When My servants ask you 'O Prophet' about Me: I am truly near. I respond to one's prayer when they call upon Me. So let them respond 'with obedience' to Me and believe in Me, perhaps they will be guided 'to the Right Way'.' [Surah Al-Baqarah, 2:186]

Dad lifted Ibrahim's chin. "Just because Allah doesn't answer our prayers the way we want doesn't mean He isn't pleased with us. His ways are beyond our understanding, son. He hears every word we speak, even in whispers."

Ibrahim felt so relieved. Uncle Farooq's words echoed in his ears. He felt ashamed that he'd doubted, even for a moment.

Dad put a comforting arm around Ibrahim's shoulders. "We may never understand why we face challenges in this life. But we have to trust that Allah, our Merciful Creator, only allows what is best for us in the end."

Ibrahim nodded again, this time with more certainty. He was determined to keep going, just like Prophet Ayyub (P.B.U.H). The path of faith could be tough, but he wouldn't give up.

## THE PROPHET's (P.B.U.H) EXAMPLE

The days that followed were like walking a tightrope for Ibrahim. He clung tightly to his father's words, using them as a shield against the waves of doubt and sadness that threatened to pull him under. He wouldn't let those feelings control him again.

He kept praying for Uncle Farooq's recovery, pouring his heart into every dua, even though his uncle remained ill. He remembered what his father had said: *Trust in Allah's plan.*

One afternoon, Ibrahim went to visit Uncle Farooq. His uncle looked frail and tired, but a small smile touched his lips when he saw Ibrahim.

"My dear Ibrahim," he whispered, his voice raspy. "Your smile always brightens my day."

Ibrahim sat beside the bed and carefully took his uncle's hand. It pained him to see Uncle Farooq so weak. He tried his best to be strong for both of them.

"I miss our talks in the garden," Uncle Farooq said, his voice thin. "But I'll get better soon, insha'Allah, and then we can sit among the flowers again."

Ibrahim wanted to believe him with all his heart. But deep down, he knew how sick Uncle Farooq was.

Uncle Farooq saw the worry etched on Ibrahim's face. "Don't you worry," he said, giving Ibrahim's hand a reassuring squeeze. "If it is Allah's will, I'll be back on my feet in no time. You have such strong faith, my boy, just like our Leader."

Ibrahim tilted his head, curious. "Who? Who's our leader?"

"Our Prophet Muhammad, peace be upon him," Uncle Farooq said, a soft light entering his eyes.

Ibrahim's face lit up. He loved hearing stories about the Prophet Muhammad (P.B.U.H)!

Uncle Farooq smiled, then launched into a story. He told Ibrahim about how hard the Prophet (P.B.U.H) worked to share Allah's message with the people, and how people refused to listen for a very long time.

Uncle Farooq's voice grew serious. "When the Prophet Muhammad (P.B.U.H) first received Allah's message, his life became full of challenges."

"For many years, he taught the people of Makkah to worship only Allah," Uncle Farooq continued. "But they mocked him and were cruel to him and his followers."

As his uncle spoke, Ibrahim pictured the scenes in his mind. He imagined the Prophet (P.B.U.H), tall and strong, his face full of kindness, patiently explaining the truth, even as people scoffed and turned away.

"But the Prophet (P.B.U.H) never stopped making dua," Uncle Farooq said. "He would ask Allah, 'Please, give me the strength to share Your light with everyone.' Even though people rejected him, he never lost faith in Allah's plan."

Ibrahim imagined the Prophet (P.B.U.H) standing tall, even as stones were thrown at him. He had no fear except the fear of Allah.

"For over ten years, the people of Makkah were cruel to the Prophet (P.B.U.H) and his followers," Uncle Farooq said. "But he never gave up hope. With every hardship he faced, his faith in Allah grew stronger. Dua was his comfort, his connection to the Divine."

Uncle Farooq paused, his eyes sparkling. "Finally, because the Prophet (P.B.U.H) never stopped preaching the truth, Allah's light shone through, reaching those who were ready to see it."

The room fell silent. Ibrahim thought about the Prophet's unwavering belief, even in the face of such hardship.

Finally, Ibrahim whispered, "He was Al-Amin, the Trustworthy One. Subhan Allah."

Uncle Farooq smiled and squeezed Ibrahim's hand gently. "Yes, dear. The Prophet's life showed us the true meaning of dua; it's about opening our hearts to Allah completely, even when things are difficult."

"We all face challenges in this life, Ibrahim," Uncle Farooq continued, his voice growing stronger. "But if we keep making dua, if we are patient and trust in Allah's plan, His wisdom and mercy will reach us. Sometimes in ways we never could have imagined!"

Uncle Farooq looked at Ibrahim, his eyes filled with love and hope. "You have that same light inside you, Ibrahim. Remember the Prophet's example whenever you feel doubt creeping in."

A warmth spread through Ibrahim, filling him with hope. He felt connected to all the Prophets and righteous people who had come before him, all those who had surrendered to Allah's will.

He looked at his uncle, his heart overflowing with love. All his worries seemed to disappear, replaced by a renewed faith and a deep sense of peace. He understood now. He understood everything.

## TRUSTING ALLAH's PLAN

After hearing Uncle Farooq's stories about the Prophet Muhammad's (P.B.U.H) incredible life, Ibrahim felt different. Stronger. More determined. The challenges he'd been facing didn't seem so big anymore.

Even though Uncle Farooq was still very sick, Ibrahim made dua with more conviction than ever. I can be strong, just like the Prophet's companions, he thought.

Every night, after finishing his prayers, Ibrahim would sit on his prayer rug, close his eyes, and picture the Prophet (P.B.U.H) and his companions, standing patiently, never giving up hope, even when surrounded by enemies.

**Prophet Mohammad (P.B.U.H) said:**

**"And whoever remains patient, Allah will make him patient. Nobody can be given a blessing better and greater than patience." [Sahih Al-Bukhari, Book 24 Hadith 548]**

"O Allah," he'd whisper, his small voice full of feeling. "Help me be patient, just like Your Messenger (P.B.U.H) was patient. Help me stay on the right path, no matter how hard it gets."

And deep inside, Ibrahim felt a warmth spread through him—a feeling of peace, of connection to something much bigger than himself. He was part of something special, something that stretched back through time, linking him to the Prophets, the righteous people, and all those who sought truth. He wasn't alone. Not anymore.

Sometimes, late at night, Ibrahim's mother would peek into his room to find him still deep in prayer. His face would be bathed in the soft glow of the nightlight, his expression peaceful and full of purpose. She would smile softly and tiptoe away, not wanting to disturb him.

It wasn't just the prayers and supplications. Ibrahim was trying hard to live according to the teachings of the Prophet Muhammad (P.B.U.H). He wanted to be kind and truthful, just like him.

Sometimes, when he was playing with his little sister, Zahra, he'd get carried away and play a little too rough. But then, he'd remember. *The Prophet (P.B.U.H) was always kind and gentle*, he'd tell himself, and he'd try to do better.

And once, when some friends wanted him to lie about who broke a vase, Ibrahim remembered that the Prophet (P.B.U.H) was known as Al-Amin, the Trustworthy One. So, even though it was hard, Ibrahim refused to lie.

Every step he took on this path—every kind word, every truthful action, strengthened Ibrahim's faith and filled him with a deep sense of peace.

Meanwhile, Uncle Farooq's illness lingered. He grew thinner and weaker with each passing day. But Ibrahim and his family never gave up hope. They took turns caring for him, surrounding him with love and prayers. It was an honor to be able to help him.

One scorching summer afternoon, Ibrahim's mother and sister were out running errands. Ibrahim and his father sat quietly beside Uncle Farooq's bed. The only sounds were the faint chirping of birds outside and the gentle tick-tock of the grandfather clock in the hallway.

Ibrahim gazed at his uncle, watching the shallow rise and fall of his chest, the way his eyelids fluttered. He looked so peaceful as if simply taking a nap.

Then, Ibrahim noticed his uncle's lips moving, trying to form words.

"Son..." he whispered, his voice raspy. "Water... please..."

Ibrahim sprang to his feet, filled the glass with cool water, and carefully held it to his lips.

Uncle Farooq drank slowly, his eyes fluttering open. At first, they seemed cloudy and unfocused. But then, he saw Ibrahim and a look of deep recognition filled his gaze.

His hand trembled as he reached out and clasped Ibrahim's small fingers. He took a deep, shuddering breath as if a weight had been lifted from his shoulders.

"My dear Ibrahim," he whispered, his voice barely audible. "You are our best example... my brave, faithful boy..."

Tears welled up in Ibrahim's eyes, but he quickly blinked them back. He wouldn't cry. Not now.

"I want you to know..." Uncle Farooq continued, each word a struggle, "that seeing your faith... it gives me peace. You remind me... what it means... to trust in Allah's plan..."

Ibrahim wanted to speak, to tell his uncle how much he loved him, but the words wouldn't come. He just squeezed his uncle's hand tighter.

"My time in this world... it is coming to an end... but I find comfort... knowing that you... will carry the light... the light of faith..." Uncle Farooq paused, struggling for breath. But his eyes shone brightly as if pouring every last ounce of his energy into these final words for his nephew.

"Ibrahim... the path of dua... it is a path... that leads us closer to Allah... closer than we can imagine... Keep that light alive in your heart... no matter what storms come your way..."

Ibrahim's father put a comforting arm around him, his own eyes filled with tears.

Uncle Farooq continued, his voice growing weaker with every word. "The challenges we face... they are not punishments... They are signs... that Allah is aware of us... that He loves us..."

"Every hardship... can be a source of growth... of mercy... of wisdom... Just hold onto your faith... Trust in Allah's plan..."

**"We will certainly test you with a touch of fear and famine and loss of property, life, and crops. Give good news to those who patiently endure."**

**[Surah Al-Baqarah, 2:155]**

Uncle Farooq's voice trailed off. He closed his eyes. His chest was still.

For a long moment, there was only silence in the room. Ibrahim and his father sat very still, holding their breath as Uncle Farooq's face relaxed and his grip on Ibrahim's hand loosened.

Then, with a final, trembling movement, Uncle Farooq lifted Ibrahim's hand and pressed it against his cheek.

"You... are the Muslim Ummah's future... our bright, shining future..." he whispered, his eyes flickering open one last time. "Thank you... for reminding me... of the way..."

His hand fell away, the light in his eyes dimming, like a candle flickering out. Uncle Farooq was gone.

Tears filled Ibrahim's eyes. His heart felt heavy with sadness. He looked at his father, who sat beside him, also filled with sorrow.

Ibrahim remembered his uncle's last words, urging him to be strong and keep his faith. It was a lot to carry, but Ibrahim knew he had to try. Uncle Farooq believed in him.

He stood slowly, his father putting a hand on his shoulder. The room felt different now, quiet and empty. But inside, Ibrahim felt a new strength growing. He would live a good life, just like Uncle Farooq taught him. He would make him proud.

# THE GARDEN OF MEMORIES

The days after Uncle Farooq passed away were very hard for Ibrahim and his family. They felt deep sadness that their beloved uncle was gone.

But Ibrahim tried to remember Uncle's final, wise words about keeping faith through life's tests.

Mother, Father, and the rest of the family helped Ibrahim feel comforted, too. They reminded him that Uncle was no longer suffering, and his soul had returned to Allah in peace.

"He walked the blessed path with conviction until the very end," Father said, giving Ibrahim a gentle hug. "We should feel inspired by Uncle Farooq's beautiful example of kindness and patience."

Slowly, the aching sadness began turning into cherished memories that made Ibrahim's heart feel warm. He remembered all the joyful times with Uncle over the years.

Ibrahim recalled Uncle's bright smile as they tended to the garden together each weekend. How he would chuckle at Ibrahim's eager questions about Allah's creations.

"The lilies symbolize the pure human soul opening itself toward the Divine light," Uncle would explain patiently, his eyes sparkling. "While the strong oak tree teaches us to sink our roots deep into faith, no matter how fiercely life's winds batter us."

Treasured moments like those lived on vividly in Ibrahim's mind, keeping Uncle's spirit alive. Each memory was a gift that filled Ibrahim's heart with light.

In the weeks after the loss, Ibrahim renewed his commitment to the blessed path more strongly than ever. He kept making dua with profound devotion each day.

Sometimes Ibrahim would gaze up at the night sky, speckled with billions of brilliant stars shining like celestial lanterns across the cosmos.

"O Allah," he would pray fervently. "Thank You for the light that guides me, even in the darkest valleys. Help me always walk the path of trust, patience, and truth – just like Your Prophets did."

Ibrahim felt closest to Uncle Farooq's memory in the beloved garden they'd tended so lovingly together. He began spending time there daily, tending the blossoming plants with care.

One sunny afternoon, Mother found Ibrahim kneeling beside the flowerbeds, contentedly running his fingers along the soft petals of a rosebush.

"Oh Ibrahim," she sighed fondly.

"He would be so immensely proud of the beautiful man you're becoming, my son," she said softly.

Whenever Ibrahim picked a juicy fig or a pomegranate bursting with seeds from the garden, he would whisper a quiet thank you to Allah (S.W.T). "Thank you for providing for us, even when I don't understand," he'd say. "Help me to be patient and trust in Your plan."

Sometimes, his little sister Zahra would tag along in the garden with him. She loved helping Ibrahim water the flowers, her giggles echoing through the air. Ibrahim cherished these moments, so full of laughter and joy.

The garden changed with the seasons, just like everything else. Ibrahim and Zahra would plant seeds together, their eyes widening with excitement as tiny green shoots pushed their way up through the soil. Uncle Farooq had taught them how to be patient, how to care for the plants, and they were learning those lessons well.

The garden was a place of peace for Ibrahim, a place where he felt close to his uncle. He would sit under the shade of the old olive tree, remembering Uncle Farooq's stories, his kind smile, his gentle voice.

It was a place where the family came together, a testament to Uncle Farooq's legacy of love and unity.

Years passed, and the garden thrived, a reflection of Ibrahim's family: resilient, strong, and full of life. Even in the face of loss, beauty had blossomed.

Enter a world where faith meets imagination in this wonderful collection of five Islamic stories. Each tale weaves together **adventure**, **wisdom**, and important **Islamic teachings** to help young Muslims navigate their journey of faith with confidence and joy.

*What's Inside This Collection:*

**"Zaynab & Zamir's Journey of Faith"** - Follow two best friends as they chase an enchanting butterfly through extraordinary lands, discovering the Five Pillars of Islam in ways that make these fundamental principles come alive with wonder and meaning.

**"Yusuf and the Lost Lamb"** - Join young shepherd Yusuf on a touching quest to find his beloved lamb Rahma, as he learns the profound power of Istighfar (seeking forgiveness) and the comfort of turning to Allah in times of need.

**"The Many Colors of Ramadan"** - Experience the beautiful diversity of Islamic traditions through Amina's eyes as she discovers that there are many wonderful ways to celebrate the blessed month of Ramadan.

**"No Two Flowers Are the Same"** - Step into Uncle Khalil's garden with Halima, Aasim, and Yasmeen as they learn valuable lessons about self-acceptance, celebrating differences, and nurturing their unique qualities just as flowers bloom in their own special way.

**"Shawana's Time Travel Adventure"** - Travel back in time with Shawana to the Golden Age of Islam, where she discovers how faith and science beautifully intertwine, meeting brilliant Muslim scholars who changed the world.

*This Collection Will Help Children:*
- Understand core Islamic principles through engaging storytelling
- Appreciate the diversity and richness of Islamic traditions
- Build confidence in their Muslim identity
- Discover the harmony between Islamic teachings and modern life

*Perfect For:*
- Muslim children ages 5-11
- Islamic schools curricula and weekend madrasas
- Family reading time and bedtime stories